WORLD CUP 86

Packed with essential information, *World Cup 86* is the indispensable pocket-companion for anyone interested in this year's tournament – whether they will be following the happenings on television or actually going to Mexico. Including:

* the Draw for the First Round of matches
* analysis of all the teams competing
* biographies of the most influential players
* Mexico – its squad, its manager, its grounds
* a brain-teasing World Cup quiz

in addition to stunning action photographs and short descriptions of the twelve past tournaments.

D1431914

Acknowledgements

I should like to thank the following who have given me facts or ideas which I have been able to use in this book: CHRIS LAWRENCE for contacting in Mexico both RUBEN GOLDBERG and the former international star ENRIQUE BORJA, ALEXANDER GOODING in South America, ROBERTO CIANFANELLI and DINO LANATI in Italy and ROBERT LIPSCOMB in France. DASHA SHENKMAN, STEPHEN BARLAY, HABS NORSTRAND, CHRISTOPHER STOBART, BRIAN GLANVILLE of *The Sunday Times*, JOHN MOYNIHAN of *The Sunday Telegraph*, ERNEST HECHT, CHRIS RHYS, KEN PRITCHARD, HARRY TATTERSALL, DEREK JANES, JOHN GILL, MANFRED HAGGAN, KEIR RADNEDGE, SINCLAIR ROAD and JACK ROLLIN. JULIET BRIGHTMORE helped me select the photographs while SARAH DAWSON and DAVID SINGER have seen the book through in a very professional manner.

WORLD CUP 86

Philip Evans

CORONET BOOKS
Hodder and Stoughton

For Harrie and Caroline

Text copyright © 1973/1986 Philip Evans

*This new edition first published by
Coronet Books 1986
Second impression March 1986*

British Library C.I.P.

Evans, Philip, *1943 Apr 4–*
    World Cup 86. – New ed.
    1. World cup (*Football championship: 1986:
    Mexico*)
    I. Title   II. Evans, Philip, *1943 Apr. 4–*.
    World Cup
    796.334'66   GV943.5 1986

    ISBN 0-340-39381-5

Printed and bound in Great Britain for
Hodder and Stoughton Paperbacks, a
division of Hodder and Stoughton Ltd.,
Mill Road, Dunton Green, Sevenoaks,
Kent (Editorial Office: 47 Bedford
Square, London WC1B 3DP) by
Cox & Wyman Ltd, Reading.
Photoset by Rowland Phototypesetting Ltd,
Bury St Edmunds, Suffolk.

CONTENTS

PROLOGUE

On 16 September 1985 a violent earthquake struck Mexico and thousands were bereaved – but for the following two weeks the world was overcome with relief as, daily, it received heart-warming reports about hundreds of people presumed to have become victims instead being found alive under tons of rubble. The eyes of the footballing world, however, were more than somewhat interested since it had been decided to ask Mexico to act as hosts to the 1986 World Cup after both Colombia, the original choice, and Brazil had declined the invitation because they were fearful of losing money.

The volcanic eruption two months later in part of Colombia was another black portent in the history of this particular edition of the tournament. (For interest's sake, Colombia came third in the qualifying group behind Argentina and Peru, went on to play in the repechage section to see which would be the fourth team to qualify from South America, but were knocked out by Paraguay, losing 0–3 away, winning 2–1 at home.) Thankfully, however, the damage to the football stadiums in Mexico was minimal since the centre-point of the earthquake was to the south-west of the country – well away from the grounds at Puebla (rebuilt in 1985) and Toluca (last rebuilt in 1970).

Staging the Finals has often known its share of troubles. In both 1930 and 1950 the Finals began with the new stadium of the hosts (Centenario in Montevideo and Maracana in Rio de Janeiro) incomplete: in 1960 Chile was ravaged by an earthquake; in 1970 and 1974 they took place two years after Olympic games that had seen great unrest – following student riots in Mexico City and the massacre of the Israeli Olympic team in Munich; and in 1978 they were used as propaganda to divert the attention of the world away from the brutal regime in Argentina.

Even though it is ridiculous to kick-off games at noon, far more is known now than was known sixteen years ago concerning the effect that playing at that high altitude will have on some of the players. Accuracy in passing remains all-important since players simply won't have the energy to hustle back in an attempt to retrieve a 'lost' ball and much greater emphasis will be placed on the area near to goal. Stories will continue to abound as to how careful the players must be with their diet lest they be struck down by a stomach complaint (like that which critically ruled Gordon Banks out of England's game versus West Germany). Given all these problems, it will be the mental attitude of the players that will be crucial.

The 1986 edition of the tournament is going to be much longer than was its 1970 relative (fifty-two games as opposed to thirty-two) but two great improvements have been made since the 1982 Finals witnessed so many meaningless games. Firstly, all the final games in a pool from the First Round will be played simultaneously (meaning that we won't have to suffer a 'fix' such as the West Germany v Austria again) and, secondly, the knock-out stage will be much longer, seeing the leading sixteen teams go forward to play Eighth-finals, Quarter-finals, and Semi-finals before the Final. We can only look forward with optimism, therefore, and hope that the 1986 Finals provide as much cultured football as did those of 1970, which were perhaps the most enjoyable in the history of the tournament.

1 A LOOK AT PREVIOUS TOURNAMENTS (1930–1958)

The idea of this book is to provide a readable and interesting guide to what we all may hope to see from what will be the thirteenth World Cup Final tournament to be held in Mexico in May and June. But before looking at some of the teams and players who may be taking part, let us look at the past tournaments.

One reason lies in the fascination with the past and the need to recognise that the great players of the past might have been truly great – whatever their date of birth! The other reason is entirely more prosaic: that of looking at power-balances. For instance, most people readily admit that the recent teams from Brazil and West Germany have had the players and methods to most excite coaches and spectators everywhere; and we must not leave out the Holland team of the past few years. But before the war Italy won the trophy twice as well, of course, as being the 1982 winners; and throughout the history of the tournament there have been strong teams from both Europe and South America.

We might point out at the start that 'the World Cup' was something of a misnomer; that its proper name during the years for which it was competed was 'the Jules Rimet Trophy'. The principle of an international tournament was agreed in 1920 by FIFA – Federation of International Footballing Associations – and although it was ten years before the first tournament came to be played, the guiding light behind the idea, and the man who most worked to get the tournament going was Jules Rimet, President of the French Football Federation. Thus the attractive gold trophy – won outright in 1970 by the Brazil team – came to be given his name. And the new trophy, won for the first time in 1974 by West Germany, was entitled the 'FIFA World Cup'.

A sense of history might help us to remember why the achievement of British and Irish football has often been so mediocre – when seen in international terms. The fact is that by 1930 – the year of the first tournament – the four British countries had

withdrawn their associations from FIFA and were thus ineligible to
compete. In 1938, it seemed the rule might be waived and, indeed,
England were invited to play the rôle of guest team – once Austria
had been overrun by the Nazis. But the offer was refused, and it
was not until the first post-war tournament came to be played in
Brazil in 1950, that any British teams took part. Even on that
occasion, the seeming obstinacy and pig-headedness of the admin-
istrators had its way! The British Home International Championships preceding the Finals was recognised by FIFA as a
qualifying group, in which the first *two* teams could go to Brazil (in
recent years the four home countries have been very fortunate to
get more than one place – the only glaring exception being that of
the 1958 Final tournaments: when all *four* home countries qualified!) The Scots, amazingly, decided that if they did not win the
title – they would not go to Brazil! The argument is one of those
nonsensical ones that ignores the large element of chance in sport
– of whatever kind. The Scots lost 1–0 to England at Hampden –
and like Achilles sulking in his tent, stayed at home to lick the
communal wound.

But this loss of twenty years – playing against the opposition
with the will to win – was something badly missed by the four
countries. If Britain gave modern football to the world then the
world soon caught up with, and overtook, us in terms of skill,
ball-control and tactics. Internationals played as 'friendlies' were
all very well but who can forget the way England players –
including Finney and Matthews – were received when they
returned from Brazil in 1950 – where they had ignominiously been
defeated by a team from the USA? And the lessons they were
shown three years later by the brilliant teams who came from
Hungary. Let alone the failure of England to qualify for the Final
tournaments of 1974 and 1978!

We have to face the fact that – as in many things – the pupil has
begun to outstrip the master; and forced him to get back to basic
principles himself. Sport – as most things – goes round in cycles,
and if it is any country's turn to get back and brush up the basic
techniques – those will stand them in good stead in years to come.

World Cup 1930 – held in Uruguay

Not unnaturally the first tournament was a strange affair. Travel to
Uruguay from Europe at the time was costly and time-consuming.
Little wonder then that so many of the European competitors
withdrew – Italy, Spain, Austria, Hungary, Germany, Switzerland
and Czechoslovakia among them. In many ways one of the stars of
the show proved to be King Carol of Rumania – he not only picked
the Rumanian team, but ensured that the players were given
adequate time off from their firms. With only France, Belgium and
Yugoslavia of the other European countries being involved, the
affair was set for a South American victory.

Why Uruguay as the place to hold a tournament such as this? It
seems strange; but the fact is that the Uruguayans had taken the
Olympic titles both in 1924 and 1928, they had promised to build a
handsome new stadium in which the games could be played and
had further guaranteed the expenses of all the competing teams.

Thirteen countries competed in four pools, the winners of each
pool moving to the Semi-final stage, together with the final played
on a knock-out basis.

When it came to it, two of the Semi-finalists could be ranked as
surprises, one as a complete surprise. That was the United States,
for so long the chopping-block for skilful South American teams
in Olympic competition, but now able to use some formidable
ex-British professionals. In their first game the Americans tanned
Belgium 3–0; then beat Paraguay by the same score and qualified
for the Semi-finals where they would meet Argentina.

The Argentinians themselves had won their group without
dropping a point, and the other Semi-finalists were Yugoslavia –
winners by 2–1 over Brazil and 4–0 over Bolivia; and the host
team, Uruguay who scratched and scraped to find their form
before going through against Peru 1–0 and then took the
Rumanians to the cleaners by four goals to none. The stage was set
for the South Americans to face the invaders.

In the event, the Semi-finals were an anti-climax. Against a skilful and ruthless Argentinian team, the strength and brawn of the United States team proved ineffective – they went down by six goals to one. And in the other game, the Uruguayans thrashed Yugoslavia by the same score.

Both victorious teams were undoubtedly strong. The Uruguayans had prepared for the tournament with a dedication that has recently been commonplace, then considered extraordinary, one that made nonsense of any thought that they were still amateurs. For two celibate months the players had been trained ruthlessly, deprived of freedom, a rigorous curfew imposed on their nocturnal wanderings. When their brilliant goalkeeper, Mazzali, was discovered late one night, shoes in hand, sneaking in after a night on the town he was thrown out and his place given to a reserve.

There has never been much love lost between South American teams on the football field, and the natural rivalry that already existed between Uruguay and Argentina had recently been pointed by the defeat of the latter at the hands of the former in the final of the 1928 Olympic tournament.

The Final, strangely, was played in a comparatively peaceful way, the Uruguayans winning by four goals to two after having trailed by the odd goal in three at half-time. Off the field and after the game came the expected Argentinian protests – that the Uruguayans had been 'brutal', that the referee had been bought. Relations between the footballing authorities of the two countries were broken off. But the first World Cup had been played – and won handsomely by a very good team.

1930 – Final Stages

Semi-Finals

ARGENTINA 6, UNITED STATES 1 (1–0)

ARGENTINA: Botasso; Della Torre, Paternoster; Evaristo, J., Monti, Orlandini; Peucelle, Scopelli, Stabile, Ferreira (capt.), Evaristo, M.
USA: Douglas; Wood, Moorhouse; Gallacher, Tracey, Auld; Brown, Gonsalvez, Patenaude, Florie (capt.), McGhee.
SCORERS: Monti, Scopelli, Stabile (2), Peucelle (2) for Argentina; Brown for USA.

URUGUAY 6, YUGOSLAVIA 1 (3–1)

URUGUAY: Ballesteros; Nasazzi (capt.), Mascheroni; Andrade, Fernandez, Gestido; Dorado, Scarone, Anselmo, Cea, Iriarte.
YUGOSLAVIA: Yavocic; Ivkovic (capt.), Mihailovic; Arsenievic, Stefanovic, Djokic; Tirnanic, Marianovic, Beck, Vujadinovic, Seculic.
SCORERS: Cea (3), Anselmo (2), Iriarte for Uruguay; Seculic for Yugoslavia.

Final

URUGUAY 4, ARGENTINA 2 (1–2)

URUGUAY: Ballesteros; Nasazzi (capt.), Mascheroni; Andrade, Fernandez, Gestido; Dorado, Scarone, Castro, Cea, Iriarte.
ARGENTINA: Botasso; Della Torre, Paternoster; Evaristo, J., Monti, Suarez; Peucelle, Varallo, Stabile, Ferreira (capt.), Evaristo, M.
SCORERS: Dorado, Cea, Iriarte, Castro for Uruguay; Peucelle, Stabile for Argentina.

World Cup 1934 – held in Italy

Four years later, the competition was altogether more representative and better attended. The Uruguayans stayed away – piqued by the refusal of so many European teams to grace their tournament in 1930; and the Argentinians, having lost too many of their star players to Italian clubs, came with something of a reserve side. More important was the background to the tournament, played in Fascist Italy. Mussolini's features stared up from the official booklets, stared down from the Tribune of Honour in the various stadia.

In the event, the Italians had a fine team, pulled together by Vittorio Pozzo, a remarkable manager. It contained three Argentinians of supposed Italian extraction – the fearsome Monti among them. They were included on the justification that if they were eligible to do military service for Italy, they were eligible to play football for Italy. From the start Pozzo proved himself a master psychologist – and he needed to be. He was dealing with temperamental stars of great technical ability in individual terms, with little will to play with and for each other. Pozzo it was who welded together a squad of seeming disparates by locking the players up *in ritiro*, forcing them to live and train closely together, matching the prima donna antics of the one against those of the other, until all came to feel that they were being treated equally. Although the strong Austrian *wunderteam* was there, although Hungary and Spain could be fancied, many things pointed towards a second victory in the tournament for the team playing at 'home'.

In fact, there were several organisational changes from the first tournament. Whereas all the games in Uruguay had been played in the new stadium, purpose-built in Montevideo, it had been realised that in future more than one city would be needed to accommodate all the games. In Uruguay, thirteen teams had competed; here there were sixteen, this complete turnout allowing a change in the formula so that the tournament was a knock-out affair from first to last; and the cities that were graced by first-round ties were eight – Rome, Naples, Florence, Milan, Turin, Bologna, Genoa and Trieste.

The gallant Americans were there, ready to prove that their performance in 1930 had been no flash in the pan; but they met Italy in the first round and lost by seven goals to one. Spain, with the fabulous Zamora in goal, beat Brazil 3–1; the Germans, another team not to be under-valued, beat Belgium 5–2; Austria scraped through against France by the odd goal in five and after extra time; and Hungary revenged the bitter humiliation of having lost to Egypt in the 1924 Olympiad. On to the second round, with Italy and Spain drawn against each other.

Zamora was much feared, a goalkeeper who in the past had too often barred the way of Italian forwards not to be taken seriously, even at his current age of thirty-three. In the event he played a superb game, plucking centres and corner-kicks out of the air with sure timing and adhesive hands. But his courage had a price to be paid. Although he withstood 120 minutes of pressure as the game – stymied at 1–1 – moved into extra time, there seemed little chance at the final whistle that he would be fit to play the next day when the replay was due to take place.

Nor did he. And although the Spanish held Italy to just the one goal, they had been forced to field five other reserves. When played, the second game was even more pathetically refereed, so badly that the Swiss official concerned was suspended by his own federation. The Italians were through, but with that smear of luck that successful teams will always need to make their point.

To join them in the Semi-finals came Germany – well organised in defence, and fortunate that the Swedes were down to ten men for much of their 2–1 victory; Austria, who beat Hungary by the same score in a brawling game that could never have suited the Austrians' penchant for swift, close passing; and Czechoslovakia, who came through against Switzerland 3–2.

That left Italy to face the fancied Austrians only two days after that bruising replay against Spain, and though there was only the one goal in their favour, their command was seldom in question. The Austrians were forced to wait until the forty-second minute before even aiming a shot at goal.

In the Final, the Italians came face to face with Czechoslovakia, much too clever for the Germans in the previous round, and were

given a real run for their money. The Czechs took the lead through
Puc in the middle of the second half, soon after missed two golden
chances and hit a post. You shouldn't be allowed such freedom in
competition, and much to their dismay the Czechs found Italy
equalising with only eight minutes to go – a freak goal from Orsi,
struck with his right foot and curling wickedly in the air. (The
following day in practice, he tried twenty times – without success –
to repeat it.) In the seventh minute of extra time, the Italians scored
the winning goal through Schiavio and that was that – victory
snatched from the enterprising Czechs just when they seemed to
have the thing in the bag.

Neutral experts were eager to make their points. The advantage
of home ground, they pointed out, had been decisive (it always is,
surely); the frenzied, para-military support; the consequent in-
timidation of referees – these all may have been decisive. They
may, but no one doubted that the 'World Cup' was now firmly
established, on the road to improvement in terms of organisation
and skill.

1934 – Final Stages

Semi-Finals

CZECHOSLOVAKIA 3, GERMANY 1 (1–0). *Rome*

CZECHOSLOVAKIA: Planika (capt.); Burger, Ctyroky; Kostalek,
Cambal, Krcil; Junek, Svoboda, Sobotka, Nejedly, Puc.
GERMANY: Kress; Haringer, Busch; Zielinski, Szepan (capt.),
Bender; Lehner, Siffling, Conen, Noack, Kobierski.
SCORERS: Nejedly (2), Krcil for Czechoslovakia; Noack for Ger-
many.

ITALY 1, AUSTRIA 0 (1–0). *Milan*

ITALY: Combi (capt.); Monzeglio, Allemandi; Ferraris IV, Monti,
Bertolini; Guaita, Meazza, Schiavio, Ferrari, Orsi.

AUSTRIA: Platzer; Cisar, Sesztar; Wagner, Smistik (capt.),
Urbanek; Zischek, Bican, Sindelar, Schall, Viertel.
SCORER: Guaita for Italy.

Third Place Match

GERMANY 3, AUSTRIA 2 (3–1). *Naples*

GERMANY: Jakob; Janes, Busch; Zielinski, Muensenberg, Bender;
Lehner, Siffling, Conen, Szepan (capt.), Heidemann.
AUSTRIA: Platzer; Cisar, Sesztar; Wagner, Smistik (capt.),
Urbanek; Zischek, Braun, Bican, Horwath, Viertel.
SCORERS: Lehner (2), Conen for Germany; Horwath, Seszta for
Austria.

Final

ITALY 2, CZECHOSLOVAKIA 1 (0–0) (1–1) after extra time.
Rome

ITALY: Combi (capt.); Monzeglio, Allemandi; Ferraris IV, Monti,
Bertolini; Guiata, Meazza, Schiavio, Ferrari, Orsi.
CZECHOSLOVAKIA: Planika (capt.); Zenisek, Ctyroky; Kostalek,
Cambal, Krcil; Junek, Svoboda, Sobotka, Nejedly, Puc.
SCORERS: Orsi, Schiavio for Italy; Puc for Czechoslovakia.

World Cup 1938 – held in France

Again the tournament was played in several venues, again it was
played along strictly knock-out lines, again it was won by Italy. And
won more convincingly, it must be said. As if to prove that their

football was the best in the world, the Italians had entered for, and won, the 1936 Olympiad – aided by the use of dubious 'amateurs', aided by the unpleasant Nazi ambience; but still a further victory to point to, further evidence that they had emerged as a powerful side.

Pozzo was still at the helm; to join Meazza in the forward line was Silvio Piola – a tall, powerful centre-forward who would score so many goals in Italian league football and for the international team; in place of the uncompromising Monti, Pozzo had at his disposal another South American hatchet-man in Andreolo of Uruguay; and to replace Combi in goal was yet another excellent keeper in Olivieri.

If victory in 1934 had been important to the Italians as a propaganda weapon, success in 1938 was deemed no less important and for the same reason. Political interest reared its head elsewhere. The Argentinians refused to come because they had not been given the competition; Spain was forced to withdraw on account of the bloody Civil War; and the Austrians – their country having been swallowed up by the Nazis – found themselves without a team for which to play. In fact, the 'German' team comprised seven players from Germany, four from Austria.

The first game went to 1–1; the replay panned out to a Swiss victory by four goals to two. Trailing by the odd goal in three into the second half, all seemed lost to the Swiss when they lost a player through injury. Not a bit of it. They waited for his return, equalised soon after, and then ran through for two more goals.

There were other surprises in store, given the context of history. The Dutch East Indies took part – annihilated by a formidable Hungarian side 6–0; and Cuba played well enough – beating the Rumanians after a replay in the first round – for us to wonder what has happened to Cuban football in the last three decades. Italy made heavy weather of Norway, winning by the odd goal in three after extra time; and in an extraordinary game, again needing extra time to decide the outcome, the Brazilians beat Poland 6–5. Playing at centre-forward for the South Americans that day – and scorer, like the Pole, Willimowski, of four goals – was Leonidas, the Black Diamond, a player of extraordinary reflex and lightning anticipation. On to the second round.

The Cubans came a great cropper at the hands of Sweden, losing 8–0; the Hungarians, with the mercurial Sarosi at centre-forward, put out gallant Switzerland 2–0; the Italians, their morale revived by the cunning Pozzo, and thanks to two goals from Piola, beat France 3–1; and the fireworks were reserved for the game between the Brazilians and the Czechs.

It was nothing less than a holocaust, with three players – two of them Brazilians – sent off, and two more retiring to hospital with broken limbs. Not for nothing was the game to be known as the 'Battle of Bordeaux', not for the last time was the tension of a great occasion to prove too much for the Brazilians. They ran out of spirit in the second half, after Leonidas had given them the lead, gave away a penalty and the world rubbed its hands or shielded its eyes in expectation of the replay.

In the event, the affair was peaceful, mild to an amazing degree. The Brazilians made nine changes, the Czechs six; Leonidas scored yet again, equalising the opening goal from the Czechs, and Roberto it was who tucked away the winner.

And then came even more crazy an episode. Drawn against the Italians, the Brazilian team manager announced that Leonidas and Tim – his two great goal-scorers – would miss the Semi-final round and were being 'kept for the final'. Nobody believed him, of course; but when the teams ran on to the pitch – no Leonidas, no Tim. *Hamlet* without the Prince and Horatio indeed; and playing straight into the hands of the Italians. They scored the first two of the three goals in the game, were seldom under hard pressure.

In the other Semi-final Sweden scored a goal within the first thirty-five seconds of play, then crumbled before the vaunted Hungarian attack, who scored five times, thrice before half-time. So dominant was the play of the central Europeans that for much of the second half a large blackbird sat peacefully on the field of play twenty yards away from the Hungarian goalkeeper.

Italy against Hungary in the Final, then; but first the play-off for third place, and the salt really rubbed into Brazilian wounds. Leonidas returned and scored two goals in a 4–2 victory over

Sweden, posing questions that might have overtaxed the Italian defence had he ever been given the chance to ask them of it, and running out as the tournament's top scorer.

The Final itself seemed to be symbolised by the struggle between two great centre-forwards; Piola for Italy, Sarosi for Hungary. For all the skill of the latter, it was the bite and drive of the former that proved decisive. Two early goals within a minute provided a dramatic beginning; then the bustling style of the Italians took them into a two-goal lead. Hungary came back with twenty minutes to go through Sarosi, threatened briefly, then went under finally with ten minutes to play when Piola drove in the Italians' fourth goal.

Italy had unquestionably deserved her triumph this time. And the World Cup would remain in Italian hands for twelve long years while the world went to war and many players of talent died violent deaths.

1938 – Final Stages

Semi-Finals

ITALY 2, BRAZIL 1 (2–0). *Marseilles*

ITALY: Olivieri; Foni, Rava; Serantoni, Andreolo, Locatelli; Biavati, Meazza (capt.), Piola, Ferrari, Colaussi.
BRAZIL: Walter; Domingas Da Guia, Machados; Zeze, Martin (capt.), Alfonsinho; Lopex, Luisinho, Peracio, Romeo, Patesko.
SCORERS: Colaussi, Meazza (penalty) for Italy; Romeo for Brazil.

HUNGARY 5, SWEDEN 1 (3–1). *Paris, Colombes*

HUNGARY: Szabo; Koranyi, Biro; Szalay, Turai, Lazar; Sas, Szengeller, Sarosi (capt.), Toldi, Titkos.
SWEDEN: Abrahamson; Eriksson, Kjellgren; Almgren, Jacobsson,

Svanstroem; Wetterstroem, Keller (capt.), Andersson H., Jonasson, Nyberg.
SCORERS: Szengeller (3), Titkos, Sarosi for Hungary; Nyberg for Sweden.

Third Place Match

BRAZIL 4, SWEDEN 2 (1–2). *Bordeaux*

BRAZIL: Batatoes; Domingas Da Guia, Machados; Zeze, Brandao, Alfonsinho; Roberto, Romeo, Leonidas (capt.), Peracio, Patesko.
SWEDEN: Abrahamson; Eriksson, Nilssen; Almgren, Linderholm, Svanstroem (capt.); Berssen, Andersson H., Jonasson, Andersson, A., Nyberg.
SCORERS: Jonasson, Nyberg for Sweden; Romeo, Leonidas (2), Peracio for Brazil.

Final

ITALY 4, HUNGARY 2 (3–1). *Paris, Colombes*

ITALY: Olivieri; Foni, Rava; Serantoni, Andreolo, Locatelli; Biavati, Meazza (capt.), Piola, Ferrari, Colaussi.
HUNGARY: Szabo; Polgar, Biro; Szalay, Szucs, Lazar; Sas, Vincze, Sarosi (capt.), Szengeller, Titkos.
SCORERS: Colaussi (2), Piola (2) for Italy; Titkos, Sarosi for Hungary.

World Cup 1950 – held in Brazil

Twenty years had elapsed since the tournament was last held in
South America, and the problems thrown up had not, it appeared,
been diluted. Thirteen teams had competed in 1930; the tally in
1950 would be no larger. The Indians qualified, but would not
come; Scotland, as we have seen, fatuously stayed out; the
Austrians were going through one of their frequent bouts of
diffidence, and felt their team not strong enough (even though
they had just beaten Italy – who would play); Hungary, like the
Russians, remained in Cold War isolation; the French, knocked
out in their qualifying group, and then reprieved, felt the journey
too long and arduous; and the Argentinians had squabbled with
the Brazilian Federation. As for West Germany, they were still
barred from FIFA.

Thirteen teams, then; and the gaps made nonsense of the new
pool system, which would apply not merely to the four qualifying
groups, but also to the final group – competed in by the four
winners. The Uruguayans, for example, had only to play one
jog-trot of a game to be through to the final pool – a victory by eight
goals to none over Bolivia. Little wonder that they seemed more
fresh and zestful in the late stages of the tournament.

The massive Maracana stadium in Rio de Janeiro was still being
built when the tournament started – and when it finished. Brazil
featured there in the opening match, beating Mexico by four clear
goals in front of a happily partisan crowd of 155,000 (the Maracana would hold 200,000). Two of their goals came from Ademir –
yet another of those incredible ball-playing inside forwards that
the Brazilians had a penchant for producing. Like the Uruguayans
in 1930, the Italians in 1934, the Brazilians had prepared with
military thoroughness – an air of celibacy and special diets reigned
supreme. They would qualify for the final pool – but not before
drawing against Switzerland with a mischosen team, and having
to fight hard against a Yugoslavian side.

Co-favourites with Brazil were – England! Appearing for the
first time in the competition, with some devastating form behind

them, the English had to be fancied. Whatever the balance of power suggested, eyes turned interestedly towards them. They had yet to find a centre-forward to replace Lawton, but Matthews was there, Finney was there, Mortensen was there, Mannion was there; and these were players whose skill was legendary. They scraped through their first game against Chile, finding the heat and humidity so oppressive that they took oxygen at half-time. And then came the shock of the tournament – possibly one of the greatest shocks in the history of international football – as England went down by just the one goal to the United States.

A number of the American players had stayed up into the early hours of the morning; several of them expected a cricket score and indicated as much to British journalists. In the event, it was eight minutes before half-time when Gaetjens headed in Bahr's cross (or was it a miskicked shot?); and that, whatever the English forwards would do in the second half, remained the only goal of the match. The victory of Chile over the Americans a few days later and by five goals to two emphasised England's shame. And although Matthews and Milburn were brought in for the final English game against Spain, although many felt the English deserved at least a draw, the die was cast. England were out of a tournament whose previous editions they had ignored, one for which they had been heavily favoured.

Into the final pool along with Spain, Brazil and Uruguay went Sweden. They had won the 1948 Olympic tournament with a team that included Gren, Nordhal and Liedholm – all, alas, now playing in Italy and blocked from selection. What irony, then, that in their first game the Swedes should play the Italians and win by the odd goal in five! A draw against the other team in their pool, Paraguay, and Sweden went through.

Little good it was to do them, with Brazil now turning on all the fireworks. In their first game the Brazilians beat Sweden 7–1; in their second, Spain by 6–1. Their trio of inside forwards – Jair, Ademir and Zizinho – seemed uncontrollable: professional counterparts of those countless boys who juggle footballs on the Copacabana beach from sunrise to sunset. Brazil, it seemed, would handsomely win the title.

The challenge came from Uruguay, held to a draw by Spain, victors over Sweden (who would in turn defeat the Spanish with that perverse logic that accompanies these affairs). If the Brazilians had Jair, Ademir and Zizinho – the Uruguayans had Juan Schiaffino, as thin as a piece of paper, a player of enormous technical skills that would later be appreciated by European audiences when he found his way into the cauldron of Italian league football, once described by Tommy Docherty as the best player he ever had to face.

But for all Schiaffino's skills, the Uruguayans were the first to admit that they were unable to match the Brazilians in terms of pure technique. Tactical expertise was needed, and tactical expertise was used. Hard as they might try, the Brazilian forwards seldom seemed able to penetrate the light-blue defensive barrier thrown up by the Uruguayan defence, the dark mastery of Maspoli in the opposing goal. No score at half-time.

Two minutes after the interval, the Maracana erupted as Friaça closed in from the wing, shot – and scored. But the Uruguayans had made their point, knew that they were able to cope with the 'superteam' that opposed them. Schiaffino it was who put them ahead, ghosting through the centre to knock in a cross. And ten minutes before the end, Ghiggia, the Uruguayan left-wing, cut in, beat his fullback to score.

The 'right team' had lost; Uruguay had won a match of breath-taking quality and the tournament for a second time after an interval of twenty years.

1950 – Final Stages

Final Pool

URUGUAY 2, SPAIN 2 (1–2). *São Paulo*

URUGUAY: Maspoli; Gonzales, M., Tejera; Gonzales, W., Varela (capt.), Andrade; Ghiggia, Perez, Miguez, Schiaffino, Vidal.

SPAIN: Ramallets; Alonzo, Gonzalvo II; Gonzalvo III, Parra,
Puchades; Basora, Igoa, Zarra, Molowny, Gainza.
SCORERS: Ghiggia, Varela for Uruguay; Basora (2) for Spain.

BRAZIL 7, SWEDEN 1 (3–1). *Rio*

BRAZIL: Barbosa; Augusto (capt.), Juvenal; Bauer, Danilo,
Bigode; Maneca, Zizinho, Ademir, Jair, Chico.
SWEDEN: Svensson; Samuelsson, Nilsson, E.; Andersson,
Nordahl, K., Gard; Sundqvist, Palmer, Jeppson, Skoglund,
Nilsson, S.
SCORERS: Ademir (4), Chico (2), Maneca for Brazil; Andersson
(penalty) for Sweden.

URUGUAY 3, SWEDEN 2 (1–2). *São Paulo*

URUGUAY: Paz; Gonzales, M., Tejera; Gambetta, Varela (capt.),
Andrade; Ghiggia, Perez, Miguez, Schiaffino, Vidal.
SWEDEN: Svensson; Samuelsson, Nilsson, E.; Andersson, Johans-
son, Gard; Johnsson, Palmer, Melberg, Skoglund, Sundqvist.
SCORERS: Palmer, Sundqvist for Sweden; Ghiggia, Miguez (2) for
Uruguay.

BRAZIL 6, SPAIN 1 (3–0). *Rio*

BRAZIL: Barbosa; Augusto (capt.), Juvenal; Bauer, Danilo,
Bigode; Friaça, Zizinho, Ademir, Jair, Chico.
SPAIN: Eizaguirre; Alonzo, Gonzalvo II; Gonzalvo III, Parra,
Puchades; Basora, Igoa, Zarra, Panizo, Gainza.
SCORERS: Jair (2), Chico (2), Zizinho, Parra (own goal) for Brazil;
Igoa for Spain.

SWEDEN 3, SPAIN 1 (2–0). *São Paulo*

SWEDEN: Svensson; Samuelsson, Nilsson, E.; Andersson, Johans-
son, Gard; Sundqvist, Mellberg, Rydell, Palmer, Johnsson.
SPAIN: Eizaguirre; Asensi, Alonzo; Silva, Parra, Puchades;
Basora, Fernandez, Zarra, Panizo, Juncosa.

SCORERS: Johansson, Mellberg, Palmer for Sweden; Zarra for Spain.

URUGUAY 2, BRAZIL 1 (o–o). *Rio*

URUGUAY: Maspoli; Gonzales, M., Tejera; Gambetta, Varela (capt.), Andrade; Ghiggia, Perez, Miguez, Schiaffino, Moran.
BRAZIL: Barbosa; Augusto (capt.), Juvenal; Bauer, Danilo, Bigode; Friaça, Zizinho, Ademir, Jair, Chico.
SCORERS: Friaça for Brazil; Schiaffino, Ghiggia for Uruguay.

Final Positions

			Goals				
	P	W	D	L	F	A	Pts
Uruguay	3	2	1	0	7	5	5
Brazil	3	2	0	1	14	4	4
Sweden	3	1	0	2	6	11	2
Spain	3	0	1	2	4	11	1

World Cup 1954 – held in Switzerland

And here was another instance of the 'wrong' team coming through to take the trophy, when Germany won their first World Cup and the brilliant Hungarians were denied their right. Bizarre organisation in which two teams from each group were 'seeded', leaving the supposedly stronger teams apart in the early stages; and the presence of a handful of really formidable teams in Hungary, Brazil, Germany, Uruguay and Austria – both these ensured that in later years this would come to be known as the last of the 'open' tournaments, the last in which teams seemed more concerned to score, than to prevent, goals.

England were there, shaky after a hammering administered at the hands of the Hungarians only a couple of weeks earlier when their winter defeat at Wembley had been exposed as no fluke. In Budapest they lost 7–1, a disorganised rabble in front of brilliant passing and shooting. History was on their side, Matthews, Wright and Finney in it; but few gave them any chance. And Scotland were also there – having repeated one part of their rôle from 1950 by losing to England; this time, however, having the courage to enter in spite of their lack of confidence.

Uruguay were strong, entering their first European tournament, unbeaten to date. Schiaffino was still there; they had splendid new wingers in Abbadie and Borges; a powerful stopper in Santamaria, later to be the bulwark of Real Madrid's invincible side. The Brazilians were slightly fancied despite being involved in a period of neurotic assessment. Their game, they felt, was too ingenious; so they closed the defence with care, came down hard on flair unless it could be harnessed to teamwork. They would wait until 1958 before perfecting the balance, but in their first game of the tournament – a 5–0 drubbing of Mexico – they introduced two great backs in the Santoses (no relation), a fine distributor in Didì, a unique winger in Julinho – a man of violent pace, superb balance, close control and with a rocket of a shot.

In *their* first game, the Uruguayans beat the Czechs 2–0; then annihilated Scotland by seven clear goals, Borges and Abbadie getting five between them. The Scottish campaign had not been helped by dissension off the pitch and the resignation, after the first defeat at the hands of Austria, of Andy Beattie, the team manager; but the Uruguayans looked good, Schiaffino in regal form. Through to join them in the Quarter-finals went Yugoslavia – who had held Brazil to a 1–1 draw in a memorable match in which their goalkeeper Beara (a former ballet dancer) had performed prodigies in defence and Zebec had given evidence of his all-round skill; England, drawing 4–4 with Belgium first time out before beating Switzerland 2–0; the Swiss, thanks to a played-off game against the Italians, who had been strangely static; Brazil;

Austria, who defeated the Czechs 5–0 with their talented half-back Ocwirk emerging as one of the players of the tournament; Germany and Hungary.

This last pair provided most of the news. The Hungarians went out in their first game, drubbed Korea 9–0; then were forced to play the Germans, the latter not having been seeded. The wily German coach, Sepp Herberger, cleverly decided to throw away this match, banked on winning the play-off against Turkey (which he did) and fielded a team largely composed of reserves. The Hungarians came through 8–3, the Germans had not given away any secrets; but most important, it was in this game that Puskas was injured, that a vital part of the Hungarian machine was put out of action.

The Hungarians had won the 1952 Olympiad; in Hidegkuti they had a deep-lying centre-forward of great verve and authority, a man who could make and score brilliant goals; at inside forward they had Kocsis and Puskas, the former a little man with the neck of a bull who could leap great heights to head a ball, the latter with a hammer of a left foot; and in the half-back line they had an excellent exemplar in Boszik, always driving forward with speed, ingenuity and strength. With four players of genius and others who were little behind, it was easy to see why the Hungarians were widely considered favourites to win the tournament.

Two things upset them. First, the injury to Puskas, who would play again only in the Final and at half-speed. The other was what came to be known as the 'Battle of Berne', a disgraceful Quarter-final tie which pitted them against the Brazilians. Hungary won the game 4–2 after being two up in the first eight minutes, after giving away a penalty, after themselves scoring from one, after Nilton Santos and Boszik had been sent off for fighting in a match that seemed more suited to a boxing ring. After the game the Brazilians invaded the Hungarian dressing-room, went berserk and came close to inflicting further serious injury on the Hungarian players. Hungary went through to the Semi-finals where they would play an unforgettable game against Uruguay, victors over an England team that fought hard, laid siege to the Uruguayan goal without really capitalising on their approach play (where Matthews was outstanding) and was let down by Merrick, the goalkeeper.

The other Semi-final would be between Austria who beat Switzerland 7–5 after having trailed 2–4 at half-time; and Germany, ploughing on with force and thoroughness against the talented Yugoslavs. In the event, the Germans 'came good' when it mattered. They scored twice from penalties in their 6–1 win, now seemed ominously hard to beat.

The Hungary–Uruguay game, even without Puskas, was a gem. Two-nil up with fifteen minutes to go, the Hungarians seemed through – until the Uruguayans counter-attacked. Schiaffino put Hohberg through, the move was repeated three minutes before the end, and extra time was on. It nearly began without Hohberg himself, who had been forced to retire 'injured' after having been overwhelmed by delighted team mates. But recover he did, to burst through early in the first period of extra time and smack in a shot – that came back off a post. In retrospect, it can be seen as the turning point; for Kocsis twice in the second period rose to head home crosses; and Hungary were through.

A Puskas far from fit, too chubby round the middle and with a sore ankle, returned for the Final. Great player though he was, the Hungarians had managed well without him, and might have done better to discard him (as Alf Ramsey would prefer Roger Hunt to Jimmy Greaves twelve years later, sacrificing rare gifts to teamwork, and win). Yet again, the Hungarians went off like a train, two goals up in eight minutes, seemingly well on the way to a victory that awaited them.

What mattered most, perhaps, was the swiftness of the German reply. Three minutes later they had drawn back a goal through Morlock; then Rahn drove home a corner; at the other end Turek remained in stupendous form between the goalposts; Rahn got the goal that would be the winner; Puskas scored – only to be given offside; and the invincible Hungarians had been beaten.

They had been beaten by a better team on the day; by the punishment of earlier games against South Americans; by a certain amount of internal dissension to do with the injury to Puskas. Yet they remained the best team that Europe had seen to date, possibly the best team that Europe has yet seen. And it took

an almost equally brilliant team from the other side of the world
and four years later, to push them into the light shadows; the
amazing Brazilians of the Sweden tournament, and their latest
wonder-boy – Pelé.

1954 – Final Stages

Quarter-Finals

GERMANY 2, YUGOSLAVIA 0 (1–0). *Geneva*

GERMANY: Turek; Laband, Kohlmeyer; Eckel, Liebrich, Mai;
Rahn, Morlock, Walter, O., Walter, F. (capt.), Schaefer.
YUGOSLAVIA: Beara; Stankovic, Crnkovic; Cjaicowski I., Horvat,
Boskov; Milutinovic, Mitic (capt.), Vukas, Bobek, Zebec.
SCORERS: Horvat (own goal), Rahn for Germany.

HUNGARY 4, BRAZIL 2 (2–1). *Berne*

HUNGARY: Grosics; Buzansky, Lantos; Boszik (capt.), Lorant,
Zakarias; Toth, M., Kocsis, Hidegkuti, Czibor, Toth, J.
BRAZIL: Castilho; Santos, D., Santos, N.; Brandaozinho, Pinheiro
(capt.), Bauer; Julinho, Didì, Indio, Tozzi, Maurinho.
SCORERS: Hidegkuti (2), Kocsis, Lantos (penalty) for Hungary;
Santos, D. (penalty), Julinho for Brazil.

AUSTRIA 7, SWITZERLAND 5 (2–4). *Lausanne*

AUSTRIA: Schmied; Hanappi, Barschandt; Ocwirk (capt.), Happel, Koller; Koerner, R., Wagner, Stojaspal, Probst, Koerner, A.
SWITZERLAND: Parlier; Neury, Kernen; Eggimann, Bocquet
(capt.), Casali; Antenen, Vonlanthen, Hugi, Ballaman, Fatton.
SCORERS: Ballaman (2), Hugi (2), Hanappi (own goal) for Switzerland; Koerner, A. (2), Ocwirk, Wagner (3), Probst for Austria.

URUGUAY 4, ENGLAND 2 (2–1). *Basel*

URUGUAY: Maspoli; Santamaria, Martinez; Andrade, Varela
(capt.), Cruz; Abbadie, Ambrois, Miguez, Schiaffino, Borges.
ENGLAND: Merrick; Staniforth, Byrne; McGarry, Wright (capt.),
Dickinson; Matthews, Broadis, Lofthouse, Wilshaw, Finney.
SCORERS: Borges, Varela, Schiaffino, Ambrois for Uruguay;
Lofthouse, Finney for England.

Semi-Finals

GERMANY 6, AUSTRIA 1 (1–0). *Basel*

GERMANY: Turek; Posipal, Kohlmeyer; Eckel, Liebrich, Mai;
Rahn, Morlock, Walter, O., Walter, F. (capt.), Schaefer.
AUSTRIA: Zeman; Hanappi, Schleger; Ocwirk (capt.), Happel,
Koller; Koerner, R., Wagner, Stojaspal, Probst, Koerner, A.
SCORERS: Schaefer, Morlock, Walter, F. (2 penalties), Walter, O.
(2) for Germany; Probst for Austria.

HUNGARY 4, URUGUAY 2 (1–0) (2–2) after extra time.
Lausanne

HUNGARY: Grosics; Buzansky, Lantos; Boszik (capt.), Lorant,
Zakarias; Budai, Kocsis, Palotas, Hidegkuti, Czibor.
URUGUAY: Maspoli; Santamaria, Martinez; Andrade (capt.), Car-
ballo, Cruz; Souto, Ambrois, Schiaffino, Hohberg, Borges.
SCORERS: Czibor, Hidegkuti, Kocsis (2) for Hungary; Hohberg
(2) for Uruguay.

Third Place Match

AUSTRIA 3, URUGUAY 1 (1–1). *Zurich*

AUSTRIA: Schmied; Hanappi, Barschandt; Ocwirk (capt.), Koll-
man, Koller; Koener, R., Wagner, Dienst, Stojaspal, Probst.

URUGUAY: Maspoli; Santamaria, Martinez; Andrade (capt.), Carballo, Cruz; Abbadie, Hohberg, Mendez, Schiaffino, Borges.
SCORERS: Stojaspal (penalty), Cruz (own goal), Ocwirk for Austria; Hohberg for Uruguay.

Final

GERMANY 3, HUNGARY 2 (2–2). *Berne*

GERMANY: Turek; Posipal, Kohlmeyer; Eckel, Liebrich, Mai; Rahn, Morlock, Walter, O., Walter, F. (capt.), Schaefer.
HUNGARY: Grosics; Buzansky, Lantos; Boszik, Lorant (capt.), Zakarias; Czibor, Kocsis, Hidegkuti, Puskas, Toth, J.
SCORERS: Puskas, Czibor for Hungary; Morlock, Rahn (2) for Germany.

World Cup 1958 – held in Sweden

The Brazilians came and conquered – came to Sweden as one of the favourites (thanks to the on-paper banality of much of the opposition), conquered with an extraordinary demonstration of prowess and skill in the Final. The backstage people concerned, for the first time, harnessed the natural talent of the players, made the team's play really effective. In 1950 the players had been allowed to express themselves too freely; in 1954, they had been too restrained. Now the blend was right.

Yet the truth remains, that like the Hungarians before them but to a lesser degree, the Brazilians proved that great teams – so called – depend essentially upon the coming-together in one period of time of a clutch of great players. Didì was in evidence again, full of lithe passes, famous for his 'falling leaf' shot – struck with the outside of the foot and fading distressingly in mid-flight;

the Santoses were playing still at fullback; and in the forward line
were two new geniuses in Garrincha and the new black prodigy,
Pelé. And there was Zagalo, a player who covered vast tracts of
ground at electric pace, one with lungs of leather and an astute
footballing brain. The components were there, and the world
waited to see whether they could be put together.

All four British teams competed; the Welsh and Irish for the
first time. The former had a fine goalkeeper in Kelsey, the majestic
John Charles, a clever inside-forward in Allchurch, an impish
winger in Cliff Jones. The latter had Danny Blanchflower and
Jimmy McIlroy, but the Munich air disaster had deprived them of
Blanchflower's brother, Jackie, a commanding centre-back. Both
teams thrived on the intimate atmosphere they created off the
field, devoid of the paranoia and bitching that had surrounded
English team selection.

To be fair to England, they had suffered terribly from Munich.
The accident deprived them of Duncan Edwards, their brilliant
left-half; Tommy Taylor, a dangerous centre-forward; and Roger
Byrne, a resourceful back. Players such as these could not be
replaced overnight, admittedly; but some of the selection was
bizarre in the extreme. Lofthouse was left at home, when his
experience might have been invaluable; and Bobby Charlton,
whose amazing swerve and lethal shooting had delighted everyone
in the previous three months, was taken – only to be left on the
touchlines for the whole tournament. Courage, it seemed, was
lacking – the courage that often wins matches and tournaments.

The Scots had eliminated Spain but lost 4–0 to England in
Glasgow. Few held out for them much hope of success. The
Hungarians had lost too many of their star players in the aftermath
of the 1956 Revolution, and such as remained were long in the
tooth. Argentina competed, but without its much-famed 'Trio of
Death' in the inside forward positions – Maschio, Angelillo and
Sivori – all playing with Italian clubs and ignored. And the
Germans seemed weak, despite the continued and cunning
presence of Herberger, the coach.

The Russians competed for the first time, having won the 1956
Olympiad in Australia. They had the amazing Yachin in goal, kept

themselves to themselves, and would play the sturdy sort of game that one has come to expect from them in recent years – functionalism with just the occasional flash of forward and midfield genius.

Playing at home, the Swedes called upon several of their stars based in Italy – the elegant Liedholm, tall and commanding in midfield; Nacka Skoglund, a hero of their 1950 World Cup team; Gustavsson, a commanding centre-back; and Kurt Hamrin, an electric little outside-right. To begin with, their supporters were pessimistic, but pessimism soon changed to optimism.

No one anticipated much from the French, yet they were to be the revelation of the tournament. In their first game, they walked through Paraguay 7–3, three of the goals coming from Juste Fontaine, who had come to the tournament not expecting to gain a place. He would score thirteen goals in all – a record that will not easily be beaten. And alongside Fontaine was Kopa – small, strong, beautifully-balanced with fine control and the ability to give a defence-splitting pass.

Group IV was the focal point – Brazil, Russia, England and Austria. The Brazilians beat the other two, drew a goalless game against England, who also drew with Russia and Austria. To a play-off, and the Russians came through by the one goal. If only Tom Finney had not been injured in the first game of the tournament. If only.

The Irish drew against the Germans, beat the Czechs, lost to Argentina – who finished bottom of the pool! They came through after a play-off against Czechoslovakia, by the odd goal in three, with McParland scoring his second goal of the game in the first period of extra time. Courage, in their case, had paid off.

The Scots drew with Yugoslavia, went down to both France and Paraguay. Better news from the Welsh, who went to a play-off in their pool against the Hungarians – and won 2–1 after trailing at half-time. The victory would put them through against Brazil, and few gave them much hope.

That especially after the 'real' Brazil had played for the first time in the third game of their qualifying group. Out had gone Jose Altafini, nicknamed 'Mazzola' for his resemblance to the great

post-war Italian inside-forward; a man who would play for Italy in
the 1962 finals, who at the age of thirty-four would score against
Derby County in the Semi-final of the 1972–73 European Cup
trophy goals that were *par excellence*, those of a venomous striker.
And in would come Garrincha and Pelé.

Both were to have an extraordinary effect on the 1958 competition, an extraordinary effect on players and spectators throughout
the world. Garrincha and Pelé – two of the great instinctive players
of the age, of any age. The former was a winger who had all the
powers of Matthews – the vicious swerve that took him outside the
full-back, the ability to accelerate into astonishing speed from a
standing start. Despite – perhaps because of – a curiously twisted
knee, a legacy from birth, his ball-control was exceptional. And
Pelé, at seventeen, his head pointed like a coconut, with all his
legendary skills already there for all to see – the ability to 'kill' a ball
on thigh or chest, to shoot ferociously from impossible angles, to
head a ball with a power that reminded people of Lawton or
Kocsis.

So what chance Wales, against players such as these? In
the event, much. If only John Charles had been fit to play, the
one Welshman who could have put pressure on the Brazilian
defence. As it was, the Welsh defence played superbly; and Pelé
was later to describe the one goal of the match as the most
important he had ever scored. And there's over a thousand to
choose from!

Into the Semi-finals with Brazil went France, Germany,
Sweden. The Germans churned on, their ageing team and cunning management able to find answers to all the questions posed
by the Yugoslavs. Sweden went through with Hamrin on venomous form – stockings rolled down, small and compact, hard to
stop once he began to find his stride, scorer of the first goal against
the Russians, maker of the second.

And there was France – the team no one was prepared to take
seriously, even though they had won their qualifying group and
scored eleven goals in the process. Against the Irish, Fontaine
scored twice more to re-emphasise his effectiveness. Tired and
depleted by injuries, the Irish had no cause for complaint. Their

effort, like that of the Welsh, had been brave and dignified.

In the Semi-finals, it was the turn of the French to suffer at the hands of Brazil. The score was still 1–1 when Jonquet, the elegant French centre-half was forced to retire in the thirty-seventh minute: a retirement that was to prove fatal as Pelé scored a hat trick and Brazil ran out winners 5–2. France would have consolation later, when they would defeat Germany in the match to decide third place by six goals to three, four coming from the incessant Fontaine.

Germany had proved no match for Sweden. The raucousness of German chanting at international matches is legendary, but in Sweden the German supporters found their match. As the Swedes progressed from round to round, so grew the noise of their fans, nationalist to the extreme. And so on the field, the Germans could find no answers to the wiles of Liedholm in midfield, the venom of Hamrin as he cut in from the wing. They would unearth a potentially great defender in Schnellinger, a powerful midfield player in Szymaniak – but the Germans knew that they deserved to be out.

In the Final, the Swedish crowd was silenced by FIFA. An official had attended the Semi-final game, put a stop to organised cheering . . . and a Swedish crowd deprived of its cheerleaders would scarcely cheer at all. Just the once, as Liedholm put Sweden ahead after four minutes. 'When the Brazilians are a goal down,' had said George Raynor, Sweden's Yorkshire coach, 'they panic all over the show.' But Raynor must have been thinking of the overtrained 1954 Brazilians or the dazzling unpredictables of 1950.

Twice, it was Garrincha; twice he swerved maniacally past Swedish defenders and centred; twice Vavà rushed in to score. And ten minutes after half-time it was Pelé's turn. Trapping a long centre on his thigh, he hooked it over his head, slashed it into the net. He would score Brazil's fifth goal with his head after Zagalo had torn through for the fourth. And though Sweden would get a second goal, that would be that.

The crowd applauded as the Brazilians did two laps of honour, first with their own flag, then with that of the Swedes. Their

supporters chanted '*samba, samba*'. And the world knew that it had
seen a new style of football.

1958 – Final Stages

Quarter-Finals

FRANCE 4, IRELAND 0 (1–0). *Norrkoping*

FRANCE: Abbes; Kaelbel, Lerond; Penverne, Jonquet, Marcel;
Wisnieski, Fontaine, Kopa, Piantoni, Vincent.
IRELAND: Gregg; Keith, McMichael; Blanchflower, Cunning-
ham, Cush; Bingham, Casey, Scott, McIlroy, McParland.
SCORERS: Wisnieski, Fontaine (2), Piantoni for France.

GERMANY 1, YUGOSLAVIA 0 (1–0). *Malmo*

GERMANY: Herkenrath; Stollenwerk, Juskowiak; Eckel, Erhardt,
Szymaniak; Rahn, Walter, Seeler, Schmidt, Schaefer.
YUGOSLAVIA: Krivocuka; Sijakovic, Crnkovic; Krstic, Zebec, Bos-
kov; Petakovik, Veselinovic, Milutinovic, Ognjanovic, Rajkov.
SCORER: Rahn for Germany.

SWEDEN 2, RUSSIA 0 (0–0). *Stockholm*

SWEDEN: Svensson; Bergmark, Axbom; Boerjesson, Gustavsson,
Parling; Hamrin, Gren, Simonsson, Liedholm, Skoglund.
RUSSIA: Yachin; Kessarev, Kuznetsov; Voinov, Krijevski, Tsarev;
Ivanov, A., Ivanov, V., Simonian, Salnikov, Ilyin.
SCORERS: Hamrin, Simonsson for Sweden.

BRAZIL 1 WALES 0 (0–0). *Gothenburg*

BRAZIL: Gilmar; De Sordi, Santos, N.; Zito, Bellini, Orlando;
Garrincha, Didì, Mazzola, Pelé, Zagalo.

WALES: Kelsey; Williams, Hopkins; Sullivan, Charles, M., Bowen; Medwin, Hewitt, Webster, Allchurch, Jones.
SCORER: Pelé for Brazil.

Semi-Finals

BRAZIL 5, FRANCE 2 (2–1). *Stockholm*

BRAZIL: Gilmar; De Sordi, Santos, N.; Zito, Bellini, Orlando; Garrincha, Didì, Vavà, Pelé, Zagalo.
FRANCE: Abbes; Kaelbel, Lerond; Penverne, Jonquet, Marcel; Wisnieski, Fontaine, Kopa, Piantoni, Vincent.
SCORERS: Vavà, Didì, Pelé (3) for Brazil; Fontaine, Piantoni for France.

SWEDEN 3, GERMANY 1 (1–1). *Gothenburg*

SWEDEN: Svensson; Bergmark, Axbom; Boerjesson, Gustavsson, Parling; Hamrin, Gren, Simonsson, Liedholm, Skoglund.
GERMANY: Herkenrath; Stollenwerk, Juskowiak; Eckel, Erhardt, Szymaniak; Rahn, Walter, Seller, Schaefer, Cieslarczyk.
SCORERS: Schaefer for Germany; Skoglund, Gren, Hamrin for Sweden.

Third Place Match

FRANCE 6, GERMANY 3 (0–0). *Gothenburg*

FRANCE: Abbes; Kaelberl, Lerond; Penverne, Lafont, Marcel; Wisnieski, Douis, Kopa, Fontaine, Vincent.
GERMANY: Kwiatowski; Stollenwerk, Erhardt; Schnellinger, Wewers, Szymaniak; Rahn, Sturm, Kelbassa, Schaefer, Cieslarczyk.

SCORERS: Fontaine (4), Kopa, penalty, Douis for France; Cieslarczyk, Rahn, Schaefer for Germany.

Final

BRAZIL 5, SWEDEN 2 (2–1). *Stockholm*

BRAZIL: Gilmar; Santos, D., Santos, N.; Zito, Bellini, Orlando; Garrincha, Didì, Vavà, Pelé, Zagalo.
SWEDEN: Svensson; Bergmark, Axbom; Boerjesson, Gustavsson, Parling; Hamrin, Gren, Simonsson, Liedholm, Skoglund.
SCORERS: Liedholm, Simonsson for Sweden; Vavà (2), Pelé (2), Zagalo for Brazil.

2 THE BRAZILIAN TRIUMPH CONTINUES – DESPITE A RUDE INTERRUPTION BY ENGLAND

World Cup 1962 – held in Chile

It should, perhaps, have been held in Argentina. But if Chile had recently had earthquakes, then the general antipathy towards Argentina in footballing circles had not lessened. And as a spokesman for the Chilean claim put it, they needed the World Cup *'because* we have nothing'. Cunning logic indeed; and the Chileans set about building a new stadium in Santiago to house a hysterical populace. (Cynics pointed out Chile had won nothing since the Pacific War in the middle of the nineteenth century.)

Brazil were the favourites, inevitably. They had two new centre-backs; and that was all. Garrincha, Zagalo, Didì and Pelé were still there – though the last would play only two games before being replaced by another exciting striker in Amarildo. And taken seriously with the Brazilians were the Russians – who on a recent South American tour had beaten Argentina, Uruguay and Chile.

England had played well on their way to Chile, beating Peru 4–0 in Lima. In Greaves and Charlton they had world class forwards; in Bobby Moore, a debutant in Lima, a defender of poise. But the self-confidence was not there, the forwards would fail time and again to find a way through the packed defences that would make a nonsense of the early part of the competition.

Italy arrived with Gianni Rivera in their ranks, arguably one of the really gifted players Europe has seen since the end of the war. Eighteen then, a precision passer of the ball and with a perfect sense of balance he would play one good game before being dropped. The Italians also brought with them a host of *Oriundi* –

foreigners of Italian extraction – such as Altafini, Sormani, Maschio and Sivori. A strong team on paper, but football matches are not won on paper – and the Italian campaign would be catastrophic.

After a goalless draw against Germany, the Italians found themselves involved in yet another of those World Cup 'battles' when they came to play Chile in Santiago. At the root of the trouble were some silly newspaper articles written by Italian journalists, critical of the organisation of the tournament, critical of the squalor of Santiago, critical of the morals of Chilean womanhood. From the start of the game the Chileans spat at the Italians, fouled them viciously. Ironic, therefore, that the two players sent off in the game should both have been Italian; while a left hook thrown by Sanchez, the Chilean winger – one that broke Maschio's nose – went unseen by the referee. Two-nil to Chile, and the Italians were effectively out of the tournament.

Germany won that second group, with Schnellinger powerful in defence, Seeler powerful in attack, Szymaniak destroying everything in midfield. They had come up with a useful inside-forward in Helmut Haller, who would find fame in Italy in later years and compete in two further World Cups. And the Chileans, inevitably, came through.

In group III, Brazil beat Mexico 2–0; were held to a goalless draw by the unfancied Czechs – a game in which Pelé pulled a muscle, and was lost to the rest of the tournament; then beat Spain, with Amarildo – Pelé's replacement – getting both goals in a 2–1 victory. The Czechs went through even though they had lost one of their games, drawn another.

In group I, the Russians won a violent yet exciting game against Yugoslavia 2–0; then were involved in an extraordinary match against the Columbians, who after being 3–0 down in the first fifteen minutes took the final score to 4–4. Yachin in goal had a sad game, sad enough for some commentators to prophesy the end of the greatest goalkeeper of modern times. Premature indeed, if only for Yachin's fine displays in England four years later. Yugoslavia would go through to the Quarter-finals with Russia, their little inside-forward, Sekularac, one of the men of the tournament.

And so to group IV, where the Hungarians looked a fine side. In Florian Albert they had unearthed a centre-forward of high gifts, another who would do marvellously in 1966. And in Solymosi, the right-half, they had a player of relaxed quality. These two were highly responsible for the 2–1 defeat of the English side in the first game; the 6–1 thrashing administered to Bulgaria in the second.

As for England, they played good football – with Bobby Charlton on great form – to beat the Argentinians 3–1. Alan Peacock made his debut, and a fine one. But in the final game against the Bulgarians, the English could find no way through a massed defence, had to be content with a goalless draw. They were through, but few would dare to class them with the Hungarians.

In the event, they met – and were beaten by – Brazil. The 3–1 scoreline seemed slightly unjust; but Garrincha was in devastating form, seemingly having added to his vast repertoire of tricks the ability to head a ball viciously. And though Hitchens equalised for England before half-time, two mistakes by Springett in goal gave goals to Vavà and Amarildo after the interval.

No surprise, that result, but surprises elsewhere. Chile, for example, came through against Russia – with Yachin still inexplicably tense in goal, and the crowd manic in its joy. Not for the first or last time, the 'home' team had confounded early prognostication.

And Hungary went out. For eighty of the ninety minutes against the Czechs Hungary attacked, inflicting serious damage on the Czech crossbar and posts. Nothing, it seemed, would ever be a few millimetres farther in the right direction; and though Solymosi and Albert did everything that was asked of them, their team ever trailed to an early, thirteenth-minute goal from the Czech inside-forward, Scherer.

In the last Quarter-final tie, the Yugoslavs put out the Germans. Only four minutes of the game remained when Galic, the inside-left, dribbled his way through the German defence and passed to Radakovic – head bandaged after a collision – to score. But the Germans could have had little reason for complaint. In Sekularac, the Yugoslavs had one of the best midfield players of the tournament; in Soskic a strong, agile goalkeeper; in Markovic, a commanding centre-back, who on the day would outplay the formidable Uwe Seeler.

In the Semi-finals, it was the turn of Chile to fall before the devastating Garrincha. He scored the first of four Brazilian goals with a fierce left-foot shot, the second with another of his new-found trampoline-like headers. And though the Chileans hit back with a goal before half-time from Toro, two further goals – this time from Vavà – in the second half, and only a penalty in return, put the Brazilians through.

Not, however, without tremblings. In the second half of the game Garrincha himself was expelled for kicking retaliatorily at a Chilean opponent; and then suffered the indignity of having his head cut open by a bottle thrown from the crowd as he was leaving the pitch. In the event, the injury was not serious, the threat of suspension from the Final very real. It was said, however, that the President of Brazil had listened to the game on headphones during Mass; that he had appealed personally to the disciplinary committee on Garrincha's behalf. The brilliant winger would play in the Final after receiving a caution.

The opposition to Brazil would be provided by the Czechs, victors in the other Semi-final against Yugoslavia. As in the Quarter-final, the Czechs had much less of the play; but this time took their chances well, scoring three goals, conceding one. Masopust controlled the midfield; the other two half-backs, Pluskal and Popluhar, sealed up the middle of the defence with rugged authority; Kvasniak ambled round in the forward line prompting and guiding. And the weary Yugoslavs were left to lose the match for third place, by the one goal and against a Chilean side again whipped on by a partisan crowd.

As in 1958, Brazil gave away the first goal of the Final – Masopust scoring in the fourteenth minute after having run on to an exquisite through-pass from Scherer; as in 1958, the team's reaction was swift and interesting. It was Pelé's replacement, Amarildo, who scored, running almost to the left-hand goal line with the ball, screwing an extraordinary shot past Schroiff, the

Czech goalkeeper, who had positioned himself perfectly at the near post to narrow the angle.

One-one, then, at half-time; and when Brazil scored again in the sixty-ninth minute, good goal though it was, it came against the run of the play. Amarildo it was who collected a pass from Zito, cut past a defender and crossed for Zito himself to charge in and head just under the bar. Thus was the slightly one-paced elegance of Masopust and Kvasniak rewarded; and salt was further rubbed into the wound twelve minutes from time when Djalma Santos hooked a centre high into the Czech penalty area, Schroiff lost its flight against the glare of the sun, lost it when it hit the ground, and Vavà snapped in to score, 3–1, seemingly a convincing win; but Garrincha had been well controlled, Didì had been obscure.

Brazil had won the Cup for the second time, but with little of the flair that they had shown in Sweden. True, Pelé had been absent for the important games, and Pelé might have made a considerable difference. The Brazilians, however, had been forced to use Zagalo as a deep-lying winger, and the 4-2-4 formation of 1958 had wilted into the 4-3-3 of 1962, would even tempt people to think of four midfield players and only two genuine strikers.

More serious, it had been a disappointing tournament. The great Puskas, taking time off from scoring goals for his new club, Real Madrid, said of the football he had seen that it was 'war'. The qualifying games had provided a string of disappointments, defensive skill had been at a premium. The tournament in Sweden had provided 119 goals, that in Chile thirty less; and where Fontaine had scored so freely in 1958, the highest figure that any individual goalscorer would reach in Chile was four.

1962 – Final Stages

Quarter-Finals

YUGOSLAVIA 1, GERMANY 0 (0–0). *Santiago*

YUGOSLAVIA: Soskic; Durkovic, Jusufi; Radakovic, Markovic, Popovic; Kovacevic, Sekularac, Jerkovic, Galic, Skoblar.
GERMANY: Fahrian; Novak, Schnellinger; Schultz, Erhardt, Giesemann; Haller, Szymaniak, Seeler, Brulls, Schaefer.
SCORER: Radakovic for Yugoslavia.

BRAZIL 3, ENGLAND 1 (1–1). *Viña del Mar*

BRAZIL: Gilmar; Santos D., Mauro, Zozimo, Santos, N.; Zito, Didì; Garrincha, Vavà, Amarildo, Zagalo.
ENGLAND: Springett; Armfield, Wilson; Moore, Norman, Flowers; Douglas, Greaves, Hitchens, Haynes, Charlton.
SCORERS: Garrincha (2), Vavà for Brazil; Hitchens for England.

CHILE 2, RUSSIA 1 (2–1). *Arica*

CHILE: Escutti; Eyzaguirre, Contreras, Sanchez, R., Navarro; Toro, Rojas; Ramirez, Landa, Tobar, Sanchez, L.
RUSSIA: Yachin; Tchokelli, Ostrovski; Voronin, Maslenkin, Netto; Chislenko, Ivanov, Ponedelnik, Mamikin, Meshki.
SCORERS: Sanchez, L., Rojas for Chile; Chislenko for Russia.

CZECHOSLOVAKIA 1, HUNGARY 0 (1–0). *Rancagua*

CZECHOSLOVAKIA: Schroiff; Lala, Novak; Pluskal, Popluhar, Masopust; Pospichal, Scherer, Kvasniak, Kadraba, Jelinek.
HUNGARY: Grosics; Matrai, Sarosi; Solymosi, Meszoly, Sipos; Sandor, Rakosi, Albert, Tichy, Fenyvesi.
SCORER: Scherer for Czechoslovakia.

Semi-Finals

BRAZIL 4, CHILE 2 (2–1). *Santiago*

BRAZIL: Gilmar; Santos, D., Mauro, Zozimo, Santos, N.; Zito, Didì; Garrincha, Vavà, Amarildo, Zagalo.
CHILE: Escutti; Eyzaguirre, Contreras, Sanchez, R., Rodriguez; Toro, Rojas; Ramirez, Landa, Tobar, Sanchez, L.
SCORERS: Garrincha (2), Vavà (2), for Brazil; Toro, Sanchez, L. (penalty) for Chile.

CZECHOSLOVAKIA 3, YUGOSLAVIA 1 (0–0). *Vina del Mar*

CZECHOSLOVAKIA: Schroiff; Lala, Novak; Pluskal, Popluhar, Masopust; Pospichal, Scherer, Kvasniak, Kadraba, Jelinek.
YUGOSLAVIA: Soskic; Durkovic, Jusufi; Radakovic, Markovic, Popovic; Sujakovic, Sekularac, Jerkovic, Galic, Skoblar.
SCORERS: Kadraba, Scherer (2), for Czechoslovakia; Jerkovic for Yugoslavia.

Third Place Match

CHILE: Godoy; Eyzaguirre, Cruz, Sanchez, R., Rodriguez; Toro, Rojas; Ramirez, Campos, Tobar, Sanchez, L.
YUGOSLAVIA: Soskic; Durkovic, Svinjarevic; Radakovic, Markovic, Popovic; Kovacevic, Sekularac, Jerkovic, Galic, Skoblar.
SCORER: Rojas for Chile.

Final

BRAZIL 3, CZECHOSLOVAKIA 1 (1–1). *Santiago*

BRAZIL: Gilmar; Santos, D., Mauro, Zozimo, Santos, N.; Zito, Didì; Garrincha, Vavà, Amarildo, Zagalo.

CZECHOSLOVAKIA: Schroiff; Tichy, Novak; Pluskal, Popluhar,
Masopust; Pospichal, Scherer, Kvasniak, Kadraba, Jelinek.
SCORERS: Masopust for Czechoslovakia; Amarildo, Zito, Vavà for
Brazil.

World Cup 1966 – held in England

When he took over from Walter Winterbottom the managership of
the English national side, Alf Ramsey promised that England
would win the 1966 tournament. They did and he did; for there
had been fewer stronger examples in the history of the game of 'the
players' manager'. It was Nobby Stiles who said it after England
had beaten Germany in the Final. '*You* did it, Alf,' he cried
tearfully. 'We'd have been nothing without you.'

England had to be favourites, given home advantage, given a
successful Scandinavian tour just before the series began. On
paper they had a fine goalkeeper in Banks, a potential match-
winner in Greaves, a gifted and well-drilled defence. But in
midfield they relied on Bobby Charlton, always known as a striker.
In the event Charlton would play superbly in the Semi-final; be
decisive in the Final. But those days were ahead.

Eyes also turned inevitably towards Brazil during their Scandinavian tour. But it was clear that the great days were passed. If
Pelé was still there, threatening as ever, there were many questions
that received unsatisfactory answers. Who would fill in for Zagalo,
with his tireless and effective running? Who was there to replace
the immaculate Didì? Was Garrincha sufficiently recovered from a
car crash and a series of serious knee operations? In fact, so strange
an amalgam was the Brazilian party between unproven young
players and older hands that they brought with them the very two
defenders they had omitted on grounds of old age four years
earlier – Bellini and Orlando.

Russia still had Yachin, still lacked the spark that makes
triumphant teams. The Italians had three stylish inside-forwards

in Mazzola, Rivera and Bulgarelli, an accomplished goal-scoring
back in the giant Facchetti. They had beaten Argentina 3–0 just
before the competition opened. But they also had a reputation for
playing below form away from home. And the Argentinians that
day had fielded something of a reserve side.

The Germans still had the indomitable Seeler up front, the
indestructible Schnellinger in defence. It was known that they
lacked a good goalkeeper, but had unearthed a fine young attacking wing-half in Beckenbauer, still had Helmut Haller to give
guidance in midfield, and in Wolfgang Overath possessed another
midfield player of the highest skill and fierce ability to read the
patterns of a game.

The Brazilians were undoubtedly drawn in the toughest group –
against Bulgaria, Hungary and Portugal. They won the opening
game, against the first of these three, lost the other two. Against
the Bulgarians both goals came from freekicks, a cannonball from
Pelé, a 'banana' shot from Garrincha; and Pelé spent much of the
match trying to avoid scything tackles.

The Brazilians then came across Hungary, losers to Portugal in
their first game thanks to some desperately inefficient goalkeeping. (More than one authority thought that Hungary would have
won this competition had they been served in goal even remotely
well.) The Hungarians had Albert, one of their heroes four years
previously; they had a fine new forward in Bene, who had played
superbly in the winning 1964 Olympic team; they had another
hero from 1962 in Meszoly, always prepared to break into attack
from behind; and they had Farkas, a deadly finisher close to goal.

Without Pelé, the Brazilians looked feeble indeed. Garrincha
looked creaky, the two elder statesmen of the defence – Djalma
Santos and Bellini – ominously static. Against fast and tricky
running, that Brazilian defence crumbled quickly. Bene swerved
and knifed through the middle after three minutes of play to slide
the ball home; and although Brazil equalised through the young
Tostao just before half-time, their goal came against all justice.

It was in the second half that their fate was sealed. First Albert
ran through, slid the ball to Bene on the right, and Farkas rushed
in to smack home the volleyed cross – as spectacular a goal as the

competition was to see. And then came a penalty, tucked home by
Meszoly. The Liverpool crowd rose to the Hungarians, and
particularly Albert; the Brazilians went back to camp to plan
survival against Portugal.

They did for this match what they might have done earlier – play
young men capable of running for ninety minutes. Pelé came back
clearly not fit, and was put out of the game early on by a vicious
tackle from Morais, one that failed to receive from the too placid
English referee the punishment it deserved – expulsion. All those
who saw it will never forget the sight of Pelé, his face agonised,
lying by the touchline swathed in a blanket.

The game against Hungary had been Brazil's first defeat in a
World Cup match since 1954 – when they had been put out in that
infamous game – by the Hungarians. The Portugal game showed
that they deserved to be out. They had no answers to Albert, Bene
and Farkas; now they had no answers to the fast running and
powerful shooting of Eusebio. It was the famous coloured player
from Mozambique who smashed in a shot in the fourteenth
minute – for Manga, the Brazilian goalkeeper to shovel it away into
the path of Simoes. A headed goal from Eusebio, then a right-foot
shot – and Brazil (despite Rildo's second-half score) were out.
They caught the train to Euston complaining – rightly – of
inefficient refereeing. But they had proved the point that great
teams are made up of great players, that greatness is not bestowed
magically from above to those countries who feel they deserve it.

Elsewhere Argentina and West Germany came through from
group II, the former gathering a reputation for ruthlessness that
would serve to dim appreciation of their undoubted skills. Both
teams beat Switzerland and Spain, their game together was drawn.
The West Germans looked classy in a 5–0 victory over Switzerland. They still had their own goalkeeping problems; but the
defence remained firm, the midfield enterprising. As for Spain,
they used their older players initially – and like Brazil came to rue
their choice. When they did put out their youngsters, it was against
the Germans and too late, despite a spirited performance.

England came through in the first group, desperately unconvincing. Against Uruguay they were unable to pierce the defensive

barrier; against Mexico it took a superb, spectacular shot from long-distance and Bobby Charlton to break the deadlock; against France they looked unconvincing against a team down to ten men for much of the game. The English defence, however, appeared impressive; fortunate indeed to have a goalkeeper of Banks' class in a year of so much bad goalkeeping. The Uruguayans beat France, drew with Mexico, to join them.

Up in the North-east it was nearly all Russia. They disposed of North Korea in the opening game, scoring three goals in the process; then scored just the one goal against a lethargic Italian team bereft of Rivera's skills. As so often Italian caution in team selection and tactics brought its just rewards. But they still had to play North Korea – a game that should have given them little cause for sleeplessness.

In the event, the game was as big a shock as England's defeat at the hands of the Americans sixteen years earlier. Though the Italians lost Bulgarelli in the thirty-fourth minute with strained ligaments (an injury caused by his own foul tackle), they through-out played like ghosts. Pak Doo Ik it was who scored the only goal of the match just before half-time, and when the final whistle came, the Middlesbrough crowd rushed on to the pitch in joy. Who could ever forget the sight of one enormous British sailor tucking a Korean player under each arm and rushing round the pitch like a lunatic. As for the Italians they went home in shame, were pelted with rotten vegetables on arrival at Genoa airport at the dead of night.

Two of the Quarter-finals remain memorable – and for totally differing reasons. The Russians won by the odd goal in three against the Hungarians, manifestly less imaginative, but having in goal a Yachin instead of a Gelei; and at Sheffield the West Germans won 4–0 against a dispirited and disorganised Uru-guayan team that had two men sent off and never really tried to stay in the game.

London and Liverpool would see the more fascinating matches. For their game against Argentina at Wembley, England left out the injured Jimmy Greaves (and were perhaps glad to do so, for his form had been disappointing) and brought in Geoff Hurst – whose last game, against Denmark, had been disastrously uninspiring. As so often happens in these things, Hurst turned out to be the match-winner, scoring the only goal of the game thirteen minutes from time; and once forcing Roma, the Argentinian goalkeeper, to an acrobatic windmill-like save at point-blank range.

Everything, however, came to be overshadowed in most people's minds by the events just before half-time when Rattin, the South Americans' captain, was sent off by the German referee, Herr Kreitlin, for objecting to the booking of one of his team mates. Rattin himself had been booked for a trip on Bobby Charlton; but though there had been many nasty and cynical Argentinian fouls, that particular one had been by no means the worst. Later the referee claimed to have sent off Rattin 'for the look on his face'. In the event the game was held up for eleven minutes while Rattin refused to move, while the Argentinian coach, Juan Carlos Lorenzo, argued from the touchline, while officials tried to get the game restarted. So the Argentinians lost the most effective player in midfield; and there can be little doubt that had they initially gone out to play as well as they could, the result might have been very different. Certainly England's eleven players made heavy work of the game in the second half against ten opponents bent merely on destructive tactics.

After the game officials moved quickly to protect the referee against the Argentinian reserves, who joined their colleagues to pound on the door of the English dressing-room, to make insinuating gestures and statements to World Cup officials. One of their players urinated on the floor outside the English quarters, their manager rubbed forefinger and thumb meaningfully together, and Alf Ramsey was distressed enough to refer to them as 'animals' in a remark that he later – understandably grudgingly – was forced to withdraw.

England were through, the mundanity of their play masked by events off the ball. And in the Semi-finals they would meet Portugal, winners against the North Koreans in a game as extraordinary as that at Wembley. After their bizarre and heartwarming achievements against the Italians, the Koreans took on Eusebio and his men, nipping about smartly. A goal in the first

minute was a fine tonic; two more soon after and the fancied
Portuguese were three down.

That was the point at which Eusebio must have realised that
Nemesis was staring him in the face. He ran through for one goal,
smashed home a penalty after Torres had had his legs taken from
underneath him, added two further goals in the second half.
Augusto got a fifth, from a corner, and the Koreans were finally
forced out, having given vast entertainment, having puzzled everyone as to the nature of their achievement. Everyone knew that for
months they had lived in solitary and rigorous confinement. But
the quickness with which they had learnt made many people
wonder whether future competitions wouldn't deserve greater
participation on the part of teams drawn from those countries with
little footballing tradition.

Given the magnificent way in which Lancashire – and particularly Liverpool – had supported its games in the competition,
Liverpudlians deserved much better than they received from the
Russia–Germany Semi-final, little more nor less than a war of
attrition. Sabo made a potentially vicious tackle on Beckenbauer –
only to come away limping himself; a long-range sliding effort
from Schnellinger on Chislenko left that Russian limping. He
went off for treatment, returned, lost a ball to Held, chased the
German and was rightly sent off by Concetto Lo Bello, the famous
Italian referee. Haller it was who scored the first German goal a
minute before half-time, just after Schnellinger's tackle; and
Beckenbauer curled a shot around the Russian defensive wall for
the second. Porkujan replied for Russia, but too late. And
although the Russian manager publicly blamed Yachin for the two
German goals, the truth was that without him they might have
ceded two or three in the first twenty minutes.

The England–Portugal Semi-final provided a pleasant and
enthralling contrast. It was in this game that the English really
came together to look formidable, the defence strong as ever,
Bobby Charlton stupendous in midfield and behind the attack in a
performance that must have gone a long way to earning him the
award as European Footballer of the Year. Everything he tried,
and he tried everything, came off. His swerving runs, long passing,

ferocious shooting – all were in evidence. He it was who scored the first goal, after José Pereira had pushed out a shot from Hunt; and just as important, every Portuguese player he passed on the way back to the centre circle stopped to shake his hand.

From first whistle to last the game was played at an electrifying pace, graced by electric skills. There was the battle between Torres and Jack Charlton, two giants in the air; that between Stiles and Eusebio, with the heart and guts of the former matched against the amazing skills of the latter; and there was the battle in midfield between Charlton and the Portuguese captain, Coluna, with his casual talent for passing, his instinctual reading of the game. When Hurst raced through eleven minutes from the end and cut the ball from the by-line for Charlton to hammer in his second goal, that seemed that. But three minutes later Jack Charlton was forced to give away a penalty, taken and scored by Eusebio. And the last few minutes were played out in a frenzy – Stiles making a fine last-ditch tackle on Simoes, Banks going down brilliantly to a vicious shot from Coluna. England were through to the Final; and though Eusebio left the pitch in tears, comforted by his team mates, he would have the consolation (admittedly small) of scoring in Portugal's victory over Russia for the third place match, and thus consolidate his position as the tournament's leading scorer.

The Final would prove as dramatic as the changes in the weather – now brilliant sunshine, now driving rain; certainly the most dramatic Final that the competition has ever seen. It was the Germans who took the lead – in the thirteenth minute after Ray Wilson – normally so cool at fullback – had nonchalantly headed a loose ball down to the feet of Haller, for the German inside-forward to slide the ball past Banks. It was a lead Germany would hold for only six minutes – until Hurst turned in a free-kick taken too swiftly by Bobby Moore.

It was eighteen minutes into the second-half before England took the lead. For much of the match Alan Ball had run Schnellin-ger ragged – Schnellinger, thought of by many as the best fullback in the world. Time after time Ball had forced him away from his touchline and into the middle, where he had been manifestly less assured. Now the small, red-haired England 'winger' forced and took a corner. The ball came to Hurst, who shot – only for a German defender to block and Peters to clip the rebound past Tilkowski, the German goalkeeper.

Pressing increasingly towards attack, the Germans were leaving themselves vulnerable in defence. Three minutes from what should have been the end of the game Hurst burst through, passed too shallowly to Charlton – whose shot was tame. And in the last minute, agonisingly, the Germans equalised. The referee deemed Jack Charlton to have obstructed Held (many thought the offence inverted), Emmerich drove the kick powerfully through the England wall, and when Held touched the ball on, Weber – the centre-half – rushed in to score.

Thus to extra-time, with both teams exhausted apart from Alan Ball, seemingly ready to run for many hours yet. Ten minutes into the first period he scampered off down the right wing and crossed precisely – for Hurst to smash a shot against the underside of the crossbar. We can now say that it was probably not a goal. But to establish that fact it took a lot of people many hours of very hard work in cinema laboratories all over the world. At the time the referee conferred with linesman – the Russian Bakhramov – and the most contentious goal of a World Cup Final was allowed.

In the last minutes, with England having hung on bravely, Hurst it was again who ran through a demoralised and static German defence to slash in a fierce shot with his left foot. He had done what no one had done before, scored a hat trick in a Final. And England, though far from being the most stylish or interesting team of the competition, had done what Alf Ramsey had said they would. They would have their critics, and many would complain about the incompetence and lack of sensibility in much of the refereeing. But the competition had been the best organised and best supported of any, and England's games in Semi-final and Final worthy to set with the best in the history of the World Cup tournament.

1966 – Final Stages

Quarter-Finals

ENGLAND 1, ARGENTINA 0 (0–0). *Wembley*

ENGLAND: Banks (Leicester City); Cohen (Fulham), Wilson (Everton); Stiles (Manchester United), Charlton, J. (Leeds United), Moore (West Ham United); Ball (Blackpool), Hurst (West Ham United), Charlton R. (Manchester United), Hunt (Liverpool), Peters (West Ham United).
ARGENTINA: Roma; Ferreiro, Perfumo, Albrecht, Marzolini; Gonzalez, Rattin, Onega; Solari, Artime, Mas.
SCORER: Hurst for England.

WEST GERMANY 4, URUGUAY 0 (1–0). *Sheffield*

WEST GERMANY: Tilkowski; Hottges, Weber, Schultz, Schnellinger; Beckenbauer, Haller, Overath; Seeler, Held, Emmerich.
URUGUAY: Mazurkiewiez; Troche; Ubinas, Gonçalves, Manicera, Caetano; Salva, Rocha, Silva, Cortez, Perez.
SCORERS: Held, Beckenbauer, Seeler, Haller for West Germany.

PORTUGAL 5, NORTH KOREA 3 (2–3). *Everton*

PORTUGAL: José Pereira; Morais, Baptista, Vicente, Hilario; Graça, Coluna, Augusto; Eusebio, Torres, Simoes.
NORTH KOREA: Ri Chan Myung; Rim Yung Sum, Shin Yung Kyoo, Ha Jung Wong, O Yook Kyung; Pak Seung Jin, Jon Seung Hwi; Han Bong Jin, Pak Doo Ik, Li Dong Woon, Yang Sung Kook.
SCORERS: Pak Seung Jin, Yang Sung Kook, Li Dong Woon for North Korea; Eusebio 4 (2 penalties), Augusto for Portugal.

RUSSIA 2, HUNGARY 1 (1–0). *Sunderland*

RUSSIA: Yachin; Ponomarev, Chesternjiev, Voronin, Danilov; Sabo, Khusainov; Chislenko, Banichevski, Malafeev, Porkujan.

HUNGARY: Gelei; Matrai; Kaposzta, Meszoly, Sipos, Szepesi; Nagy, Albert, Rakosi; Bene, Farkas.
SCORERS: Chislenko, Porkujan for Russia; Bene for Hungary.

Semi-Finals

WEST GERMANY 2, RUSSIA 1 (1–0). *Everton*

WEST GERMANY: Tilkowski; Hottges, Weber, Schultz, Schnellinger; Beckenbauer, Haller, Overath, Seeler, Held, Emmerich.
RUSSIA: Yachin; Ponomarev, Chesternjiev, Voronin, Danilov; Sabo, Khusainov; Chislenko, Banichevski, Malafeev, Porkujan.
SCORERS: Haller, Beckenbauer for Germany; Porkujan for Russia.

ENGLAND 2, PORTUGAL 1 (1–0). *Wembley*

ENGLAND: Banks (Leicester City); Cohen (Fulham), Wilson (Everton); Stiles (Manchester United), Charlton, J. (Leeds United), Moore (West Ham United); Ball (Blackpool), Hurst (West Ham United), Charlton, R. (Manchester United), Hunt (Liverpool), Peters (West Ham United).
PORTUGAL: José Pereira; Festa, Baptista, Carlos, Hilario; Graça, Coluna, Augusto; Eusebio, Torres, Simoes.
SCORERS: Charlton, R. (2) for England; Eusebio (penalty) for Portugal.

Third Place Match

PORTUGAL 2, RUSSIA 1 (1–1). *Wembley*

PORTUGAL: José Pereira; Festa, Baptista, Carlos, Hilario; Graça, Coluna, Augusto; Eusebio, Torres, Simoes.
RUSSIA: Yachin; Ponomarev, Khurtsilava, Korneev, Danilov;

Voronin, Sichinava; Metreveli, Malafeev, Banichevski, Sere-
brianikov.
SCORERS: Eusebio (penalty), Torres for Portugal; Malafeev for
Russia.

Final

ENGLAND 4, WEST GERMANY 2 (1–1) (2–2) after extra
time. *Wembley*

ENGLAND: Banks; Cohen, Wilson; Stiles, Charlton, J., Moore;
Ball, Hurst, Charlton, R., Hunt, Peters.
WEST GERMANY: Tilkowski; Hottges, Schultz; Weber, Schnellin-
ger, Haller; Beckenbauer, Overath, Seeler, Held, Emmerich.
SCORERS: Hurst (3), Peters for England; Haller, Weber for
Germany.

World Cup 1970 – held in Mexico

Given that the tournament tended to be played alternately in
Europe and South America, it was inevitable that Mexico would be
a venue sooner or later. For many, however, the 'later' would have
been preferable. The 1968 Olympiad had shown precisely and
agonisingly the problems thrown up in expecting top-class athletes
to compete at high altitudes. And few parts of central Mexico were
at less than 6–7,000 feet above sea level. The nonchalant could at
least pretend that it made life more interesting.

What could have been prevented – and wasn't – was the callous
selling-out of the tournament to financial interests. Too many
games were played in noonday heat – merely to satisfy European
television companies eager to televise games at peak viewing times.
England, for example, played their vital group match against Brazil

at noon, in temperatures of nearly 100 degrees and there was barely an England player who had not lost eight or ten pounds in weight as a result of dehydration.

England's preparations had been thorough enough. The team arrived in Mexico well before the tournament started; good accommodation had been found; supplies of food and drink had been flown out (though the Mexican customs officials appeared un-cooperative at first); the players were even supplied with reading material by Coronet Books, one of the country's leading paperback publishing firms. Leaving Mexico for a short tour, England won handsome victories over Columbia and Ecuador, the defence seemingly as ungenerous as it had been in 1966.

It was after the second of these games, as the team stopped off in Bogota on the way back to Mexico that Bobby Moore, the English captain, was absurdly accused of having stolen a bracelet from a hotel jewellers. Much has been written about this extraordinary incident, that would last for nearly two years, until the 'charges' were finally dropped. The important point to underline is Moore's amazing coolness during the whole affair. In a situation where many players might have cracked under the nervous strain imposed by being unable to fly back to Mexico with the rest of the team, of having to remain in a state of semi-solitary confinement while the matter was tentatively cleared up Moore was simply magnificent. Within days he was to go out and prove to the world that, as in 1966, he remained the best defensive wing-half in modern football.

If England had Moore, then Brazil still had Pelé. The Brazilians had taken, only months before the Finals, the extraordinary step of sacking their manager, the bubbling Joao Saldanha, and replacing him with Mario Zagalo, one of the heroes of 1958 and 1962. No one doubted the Brazilian talent. If they had a goalkeeper of laughable mediocrity in Felix, if their defence seemed unsound – then they had Gerson in midfield and up front Jairzinho and Tostao. The latter had recently undergone eye surgery, but was known to be a formidable foil to Pelé. The first few games would tell all about Brazil.

The West Germans were there also, eager for the chance to

revenge their defeat at the hands of the English four years
previously. The bulk of that side remained; they had two incisive
wingers in Grabowski and Libuda, a 'new' goalkeeper in Maier,
one of the best of the tournament. And that is not meant dispara-
gingly. One of the many contrasts between the 1966 competition
and that to be held in Mexico would be the overall improvement in
goalkeeping standards. Banks (England), Kavazashvili (Russia),
Piot (Belgium), Calderon (Mexico), Albertosi (Italy) and Mazurkiewicz (Uruguay) – all, with Maier, kept goal well in conditions
that were far from helpful, ones in which the ball moved fast
through the rarefied air, swerving and dipping unexpectedly, ones
in which the brightness of the light put a premium on good
judgement. We might note here that the fearsome Gerd Muller,
who would score most goals in the tournament, came to face only
two of the above-mentioned, when Germany played their Semi-
final against Italy and their final game against Uruguay.

The Italians came strangely, having qualified with some ease
against East Germany and Wales in their preliminary group. In
Riva they had a striker of renown, his left foot a terrifying weapon
when given the chance to exercise itself. But too often Riva's
brilliant goals had camouflaged weaknesses in the defence, lack of
understanding in midfield. Mazzola was there for the second time,
Rivera for the third – both players of high technical accomplishment, and supposedly unable to play together. The Italians decided in favour of the *staffeta*, a system whereby Mazzola would
play the first half of each game, Rivera the second. The latter
found it unacceptable, said so loudly, was nearly sent home as
punishment, stayed, and in two games at least, would prove that he
is one of the world's great intuitive players.

The Russians looked solid as ever, with Kavazashvili a worthy
successor in goal to the great Yachin, and Shesternev a sweeper
little behind Bobby Moore in terms of technical expertise and
tactical acumen. They had an interesting young striker in
Bishovets, but would play a type of football that lacked genuine
inventiveness. Uruguay were another team strong on paper, again
served brilliantly in goal (by Mazurkiewicz, one of the very small
clutch of good goalkeepers four years previously), and with some

terrifyingly robust defenders. One remembers particularly Montero Castillo in the centre of the field, Ubinas and Ancheta elsewhere. And the joker in the pack had to be Peru, coached for the tournament by Didì, the Brazilian ex-player and perennial hero of 1954, 1958 and 1962. It was known that they had some forwards of dazzling technical gifts, but did they have a team, could they put together a game?

Generally speaking those teams that were expected to come through came through. The first game of the first group – and the tournament – was that between Mexico (the hosts) and Russia. A goalless draw, as with its 1966 counterpart, sounded an ominous warning. But Belgium played some light, waltzing football to beat El Salvador the following day; and when they came to meet Russia, deserved better than the 4–1 defeat that they allowed to be inflicted upon them. Bishovets scored two of those goals, Shesternev marshalled the defence superbly; and it was one of those days when the Russians showed the world just what they could do when prepared to cast off thoughts of weighty preparation and over-drilled tactics. And in the final game of the group, the Mexicans went through against the Belgians 1–0, thanks to a hotly disputed penalty decision, one that seemed to have been not uninfluenced by the frenzy of a vast home crowd. Mexico, unconvincingly, and Russia through, then, from that group.

Group II looked good for both Italy and Uruguay. Israel looked too raw, Sweden – despite the presence of one or two players of high talent, such as Kindvall and Grahn, who played their club football outside Sweden – lacked strength in depth. They it was who first faced Italy, going down to a drive from some long range delivered by the Italian midfield player, Domenghini, who throughout the tournament would play with a ubiquity that periously ignored the heat of the sun and the rarity of the air. The Uruguayans scraped through 2–0 against Israel, more importantly lost Pedro Rocha, their midfield general after only a few minutes of play. It was an injury that would force the South American team even further back on to their defensive and uncompromising heels, for Rocha would take no further part in the tournament.

The next match brought these two teams together into a goalless draw, with both sets of players full of hostility (both masked and overt). Riva was to claim that from the first Uruguayan defenders had spat at him whenever they were close; which did not excuse his lethargy. More dreary football was to follow, and the results continued to prove evidence of the essentially defensive attitudes that permeated group matches. The Swedes beat the Uruguayans, who went through on a marginally better goal average; and the Italians got through with two goalless draws and that one win. Top of the group with only one goal in three matches: that, surely, couldn't be the stuff of which world champions were made?

Group III was, indubitably, the toughest on paper; and certainly the matches from that group provided some of the most fascinating football. If the English won their first game against Rumania, they did so with some lack of ease, thanks to a goal from Geoff Hurst in the seventieth minute, and despite some sadistic tackling by the Rumanian defenders, a certain Mocanu in particular. If the Brazilians appeared to thrash the Czechs 4–1, it must be remembered that Petras scored the first goal of the match for Czechoslovakia, that they were served with some indifferent goalkeeping, that the third Brazilian goal (scored by Jairzinho) looked suspiciously offside. But Pelé was on superb form, scored an extraordinary goal; Rivelino put another in from a swerving free-kick; Jairzinho scored again, always threatened when he had possession; and Gerson in midfield sprayed accurate passes around with high panache, underlining the thought that so many of the world's finest distributors have been players whose athleticism was far from robust. Gerson, for example, is something of a one-paced player (and that pace never faster than slow-medium) who is a compulsive cigarette smoker. Hardly the stuff of which the textbook heroes are made, but a player of great influence.

Too many people – and particularly in England – have tended to overlook the fact of Gerson's absence when England came to play Brazil. That is not to say that England didn't play thoroughly well, that they did not suggest themselves as one of the two or three best teams of the tournament during that game. It was a classic, worthy to enter the Pantheon of brilliant World Cup games. The English had gone to Mexico in the rôle of villains, with too many people

disgruntled as to the manner of their victory four years earlier; and
this animosity was to manifest itself at every turn. The night before
the Brazil game a crowd several thousand strong milled round the
Hilton Hotel, where they were staying, and contrived to make
enough noise to prevent the players getting any sleep. Many admitted afterwards that they had for long minutes and hours simply
stood by the windows of their rooms, staring at the crowd below,
and at the inability of the Mexican police to deal with the problem.

They then went out at midday, in scorching heat that
approached 100 degrees of Fahrenheit and played Brazil off the
pitch for long stretches of the game. Mullery played brilliantly,
policing Pelé with scrupulous toughness. True, Pelé got away
from him in the early minutes of the game after Jairzinho had
rounded Cooper on England's left and smacked across a perfect
centre; up went Pelé, down came the ball, and down also came
Gordon Banks to scoop the ball up with his right wrist – a save that
must rank with the very best in the history of the World Cup tournament. Otherwise Pelé was kept moderately quiet; and Moore
at the heart of the defence gave further evidence that he was the
best defensive player in the world, his timing of the tackle precise,
his reading of the game astute, his distribution imaginative.

The only goal of the match (perfect evidence that goals in
themselves do not exciting football make) came after fourteen
minutes of the second half, after Tostao had teased the left of the
English defence and slid the ball across goal for Jairzinho to score.
The truth was, however, that if Banks was forced to at least three
other saves of high quality, England were given, and missed, a
plentitude of chances at the other end. Ball hit the bar, missed
another good chance; Astle blazed wide after being put into an
attractive position; Hurst might have had a goal, but shot feebly at
the crucial moment. If the style is the man, then the style must also
be the game; and yet again we were left to ponder that one of the
essential weaknesses of the English game was its lack of high
technical accomplishment – where the world's best strikers would
snap up chances with glee, too often English forwards had not the
basic 'killer' instinct that comes hand in hand (or foot to foot) with
technical prowess.

The Brazilians went on to beat the Rumanians, again despite the deprivation of Gerson; and, on this occasion, that of Rivelino. England drafted in a handful of 'reserves' for the game against the Czechs, played badly, won through a disputed penalty; and joined Brazil in the Quarter-finals.

In group IV were the mysterious Peruvians. In their first game, they fell behind to Bulgaria, conceded two goals from set pieces; and then in the second half turned on their skills. Many were quick to compare them with the Brazilians in their flamboyance, their brilliant control. In defence they had a sturdy player in Chumpitaz, some imaginative forwards in Gallardo, Sotil, Cubillas and Baylon; and in the space of twenty minutes turned the two-goal deficit into a 3–2 score that would last until the game's finish.

That would prove to be the decisive game in the group. For although they fared poorly against Morocco in their first match, the West Germans seemed certainties for qualification; a thought that was reinforced when they came to play the Bulgarians in turn. Though the East Europeans scored first through Nikodimov (following a free kick), the Germans ran in five goals, three of them going to Muller. Libuda was on venomous form on their right, Muller and Seeler brave and energetic in the middle. In fact Muller would score another hat trick when the Germans came to meet Peru a few days later, marching firmly along the road that would make him the tournament's highest scorer. Despite that 3–1 defeat, Peru would qualify.

No goal Muller scored in the competition was, however, more important than that he slashed home in the Quarter-final tie that followed, when the Germans were drawn against England. It was a game England could, and should, have won. For a team of their defensive prowess to lead by two clear goals and eventually lose by the odd score in five was remarkable. It is too easy to blame Peter Bonetti, drafted into the goalkeeping position after Banks had been forced to withdraw with a stomach complaint of mysterious origin. Banks may well have saved two of the three German goals

---

* Soon after the Peruvians arrived an earthquake ravaged their country, killing thousands.

to be scored; but there were other, better reasons to explain the collapse.

England's lead came through Mullery – racing through to exchange passes with Lee, sliding the ball out to Newton on the right, smashing home the perfect cross; and Peters – knocking in another fine cross from Newton. That left England two up after five minutes of the second half, and seemingly set for a good win. And then came the substitutions – Grabowski on for Libuda; Bell and Hunter on for Charlton and Peters – that were to prove decisive. While Charlton remained, Beckenbauer, his policeman, stayed quiet; without further patrolling duties, Beckenbauer cut loose, scored the first, important, German goal. Where Cooper had controlled Libuda on the left, he now found Grabowski irrepressible. Although Hurst nearly made the score 3–1 with a fine low header, it was the Germans who came through, Seeler backheading a long cross from Schnellinger.

As in the 1966 Final, the game between the two countries entered extra time, with the crowd noisily pro-German, and England's defence looking increasingly tired. Hurst scored – to be given, mysteriously, offside. And then came the deciding goal – Grabowski winning control on the right, punting over a cross, which Muller tucked away as the ball was nodded down to him. England were out of the competition, after having controlled vast stretches of their games against Brazil and West Germany, after having suggested themselves strongly as possible opposition for Brazil in the Final.

Through into the Semi-finals with Germany would go Italy, Brazil and Uruguay. The last won through in the final moments of extra time in a hard game against the Russians, and with a hotly disputed goal into the bargain. But the Russians had missed too many chances to have reason for bitter complaint.

Brazil went through, now with both Rivelino and Gerson back in the side, and at the expense of Peru to the tune of 4–2. Gallardo scored two goals for the entertaining Peruvians, but they were up against a side that knew their own footballing language and were more adept practitioners.

And Italy went through, stuttering for much of their game

against Mexico, until Gianni Rivera made his appearance at the start of the second half and suggested openings for his compatriots. Riva scored twice, delighting those who knew his prowess and were still waiting patiently for evidence of its existence; and there was a goal from Rivera himself, nice ammunition for those who felt that Italy were squandering his exquisite talents, that there should always have been a place for him in that team, with or without the brave resourceful Sandro Mazzola.

The Semi-final draw – Brazil against Uruguay, Italy against West Germany – promised, and delivered, much. The first of these games pitted the resource of the Brazilian midfield and attack against the misanthropy of the Uruguayan defence, with its squad of muscular central defenders. In the event, it was Uruguay who scored first, through Cubilla (as opposed to Cubillas, the Peruvian), and though Brazil equalised just before half-time through Clodoaldo, the important second goal did not materialise until fourteen minutes before the end, when Jairzinho danced past three defenders on the right and drove the ball home from a sharp angle. A goal from Rivelino in the last second of the game gave the scoreline a lopsided quality that was grossly unfair to the courage and ingenuity of much of the Uruguayan play, still deprived of the skills of the injured – and potentially influential – Pedro Rocha.

But Italy against West Germany – that was really something of a collector's item. It was an interesting comment on the Italian footballing mentality that after a game of thrilling interest, despite the fact that their team had been victorious, many Italian commentators would dismiss it as being something of a circus turn on the grounds that neither of the two defences was good enough. In fact, Italy created much of their good fortune early in the game when a bad tackle by Bertini left the elegant Beckenbauer with an injured arm. He would play much of the game at strolling pace and in some pain, his arm strapped to his chest.

The Italians took the lead after only seven minutes, Boninsegna clearing Riva out of his way to plant a left-footed shot firmly past Maier. Given the Italian penchant for defensive expertise, the Germans must have known that they had a titanic struggle on their hands, and well though they played against the cautious Italians in

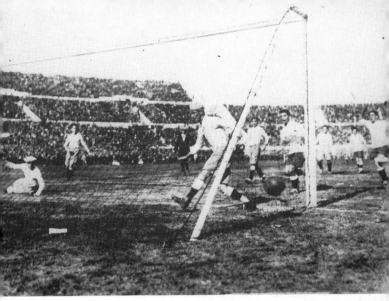

The last moments of the 1930 Final in which Uruguay beat
Argentina 4-2, the scorer being Hector Castro (just to the left of
the right-hand upright), who was known as 'El Manco' after his
right arm had been amputated at the elbow.

The only goal of the Semi-final in the 1934 World Cup in which
Italy beat Austria, scored by Enrico Guiata. Italy went on to win
the Final against Czechoslovakia 2-1 after extra time had been
played.

Italy triumph again in 1938 by beating Hungary 4-2. Holding the Jules Rimet trophy is their manager, Vittorio Pozzo, and just to *his* left is Silvio Piola, who scored twice in the Final.

The 1950 World Cup and Uruguay's goalkeeper, Roque Maspoli, manages to dive down to the ball before Brazil's forward, Ademir, can reach it. Uruguay won the match 2-1, although Brazil had 'home' advantage, and thus took the title for the second time.

Max Morlock (West Germany) slides the ball under the arms of the advancing Hungarian goalkeeper, Gyula Grosics, to score his side's first goal in the 'unexpected' 3-2 victory in the 1954 Final.

Harry Gregg (Northern Ireland) fails to stop a shot by Uwe Seeler (West Germany), in a group match from the 1958 World Cup which finished in a 2-2 draw.

Kalle Svensson dives to prevent trouble from John Charles during the goalless draw in the 1958 tournament between Sweden and Wales.

From the 1958 Final. The electrifying Garrincha centres for Vavà to strike home Brazil's first, and equalising, goal in the 5-2 defeat of Sweden.

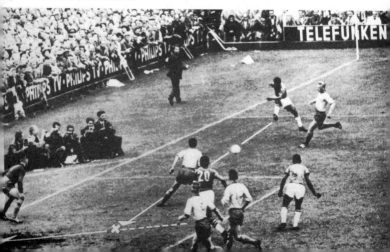

Luis Suarez (Spain) trying to find a way through an uncompromising Czechoslovakian defence during the 1962 World Cup, which his side lost just by the one goal. Czechoslovakia proceeded to the Final.

The Brazilian team before the 1962 Final in which they beat Czechoslovakia 3-1. *Top (left to right):* Djalma Santos, Zito, Gilmar, Mauro, Nilton Santos and Zozimo. *Bottom:* Garrincha, Didi, Vavà, Amarildo and Zagalo.

Brazil against Hungary in 1966 and Jairzinho attempts a
header which the Hungarian goalkeeper, Jozsef Gelei, manages
to save. It was a memorable match which Hungary won 3-1.

Russia versus Hungary Quarter-final in 1966 which Russia won
2-1. Here Ferenc Bene (second from left) scores Hungary's only
goal.

1966 Quarter-final between England and Argentina. Referee Kreitlen orders off Antonio Rattin after he had objected to the 'booking' of a colleague. Play was held up for ten minutes in which time the Argentinians petitioned, argued and at one time appeared ready to leave the field *en masse*.

Third Place match in 1966 between Portugal and Russia. Eusebio (Portugal) forces his way through the Russian defence only to see his shot saved by Lev Yachin. Despite this, Portugal won 2-1 and Eusebio finished as the highest scorer in the tournament.

1966 Final and Wolfgang Weber scores in the final minute of
normal time. Also in the picture are Uwe Seeler, George Cohen,
Bobby Moore, Ray Wilson, Kurt Schnellinger, Jackie Charlton
and Gordon Banks (the goalkeeper).

Geoff Hurst (England) makes sure of victory in the 1966 Final
by driving home the fourth goal in England's 4-2 victory over
West Germany. The German player is Wolfgang Overath.

the second half, too many chances went begging. Indeed it was not
until the third minute of injury time that Schnellinger, the German
sweeper (and ironically he served brilliantly in that rôle at club
level for AC Milan), came forward to slide the ball home after
Grabowski had crossed from the left.

Into extra-time, and on came the nervousness and the mistakes.
The Germans went ahead after five minutes through Muller;
Burgnich came up to knock in Rivera's free kick; Riva scored a fine
goal with that formidable left foot of his – and the first period of
extra-time ended with Italy leading 3–2. The Italians were pulled
back again soon after the resumption of play, when Muller dived
low to head home; and then came the decisive goal, with the
talented Boninsegna taking the ball out to the left, leaving his
opponent Schulz on his bottom, and crossing for Gianni Rivera to
drive the ball precisely into goal. Once again Rivera had missed the
first forty-five minutes; once again he had been decisive in the later
stages of a game. The Italians were through, not remotely the
second best side in the tournament, but undoubtedly one of high
technical accomplishment, and in that Semi-final game, having
given the lie to those detractors eager to claim that Italian teams
always lack fire and spirit.

In the play-off for third place the Germans did what the Italians
had failed to do – and beat Uruguay. They did so with a fine goal
scored by Overath after a thrilling movement that involved Libuda, Muller and Seeler. There was entertaining action at both ends,
with Mazurkiewicz and Walter (the young German goalkeeper)
both being forced to fine saves. But a match of technical adroitness
could not raise the crowd – which, like the televised world, awaited
the Final itself.

Brazil won it, and won it handsomely. They did so with football
of assured fluency, they did it by underlining brilliantly, and
against the master exponents of defensive football, all the old
clichés about attack being the best means of defence. Of the
Italians Sandro Mazzola covered vast tracts of ground, played with
authority and spirit; Boninsegna showed what a dangerous striker
he could be, given even a few metres of space; Facchetti strove
manfully against Jairzinho. But much of the marking was sloppy on

the one hand, crude on the other; and there was about the team as a whole a curious refusal to play with any real vestige of self-confidence.

It was, fittingly, Pelé who gave the Brazilians the lead after eighteen minutes, heading down Rivelino's cross; if the great man had a comparatively human game, then his presence and brilliance had given the tournament as a whole a fine streak of class. And no one looked more bemused than he when the Italians equalised a few minutes before half-time through Boninsegna and after a silly back-pass by Clodoaldo had left Felix stranded outside the Brazilian goal.

That was delusion indeed, for in the second half the Brazilians made heavy amends. Gerson, who throughout played with a majesty that capitalised on the failure of the Italian midfield, was the scorer of the second of the four Brazilian goals, his left foot curling in a fine shot from distance. Jairzinho it was who scored the third, slipping in a pass from Pelé and setting a new record by virtue of having scored in all six games in which he played; and the Italians were a thoroughly demoralised side by the time Carlos Alberto came through down the right touchline to crash the ball in after an exquisitely weighted pass from Pelé had put him through in the last few minutes of the game.

The Italians brought on Juliano for the ineffectual Bertini; with six minutes to go, bizarrely substituted Rivera for Boninsegna – a move that was staggering in its lack of logic. Had Rivera appeared earlier, in place of the tired Domenghini, one might have seen the point, he might have effected something of a rescue. But the ship had been truly sunk; despite their appearance in the Final the Italians would go home and indulge in the most Machiavellian post-mortems. And by virtue of their third victory, the Brazilians would appropriate the Jules Rimet trophy.

It was a popular victory, a welcome evidence that attacking football and intuitive genius still had their place in a footballing world obsessed by 'work-rate' and (often) skill-less hard running. Winning the tournament in 1966 England had conceded only three goals, scored eleven. Four years later, the Brazilians had triumphed by conceding seven goals and scoring nineteen. Either

England or West Germany – not to mention Uruguay – might have
made of the Final more than did the Italians. And it remained true
(as it may always remain true) that some of the refereeing left much
to be desired. But Ferenc Puskas, and many other great stars of the
past, would have approved. The football of the Brazilians was
many miles removed from the 'war' that people had gloomily
forecast as being the only result of international competition.
Above all, the Brazilians made the thing look enjoyable, had
helped to restore that enthusiasm without which sport in any form
will wither away. More chants of *'samba'*, and the spectacle of the
greatest player of that, or any, generation – Pelé – being raised
aloft by delighted Brazilian fans.

1970 – Final Stages

Quarter-Finals

WEST GERMANY 3, ENGLAND 2 (0–1) (2–2) after extra
time. *Leon*

WEST GERMANY: Maier; Schnellinger, Vogts, Fichtel, Hottges
(Schulz); Beckenbauer, Overath, Seeler; Libuda (Grabowski),
Muller, Loehr.
ENGLAND: Bonetti (Chelsea); Newton (Everton); Cooper (Leeds
United); Mullery (Spurs), Labone (Everton), Moore (West Ham
United); Lee (Manchester City), Ball (Everton), Hurst (West
Ham United), Charlton (Manchester United) [Bell (Manchester
City)], Peters (Spurs) [Hunter (Leeds United)].
SCORERS: Mullery, Peters for England; Beckenbauer, Seeler,
Muller for West Germany.

BRAZIL 4, PERU 2 (2–1). *Guadalajara*

BRAZIL: Felix; Carlos Alberto, Brito, Piazza, Marco Antonio;
Clodoaldo, Gerson (Paulo Cesar); Jairzinho (Roberto), Tostao,
Pelé, Rivelino.

PERU: Rubiños; Campos, Fernandez, Chumpitaz, Fuentes; Mifflin, Challe; Baylon (Sotil), Perico Leon (Eladio Reyes), Cubillas, Gallardo.
SCORERS: Rivelino, Tostao (2), Jairzinho for Brazil; Gallardo, Cubillas for Peru.

ITALY 4, MEXICO 1 (1–1). *Toluca*

ITALY: Albertosi; Burgnich, Cera, Rosato, Facchetti; Bertini, Mazzola (Rivera), De Sisti; Domenghini (Gori), Boninsegna, Riva.
MEXICO: Calderon; Vantolra, Pena, Guzman, Perez; Gonzales (Borja), Pulido, Munguia (Diaz); Valdivia, Fragoso, Padilla.
SCORERS: Domenghini, Riva (2), Rivera for Italy; Gonzales for Mexico.

URUGUAY 1, RUSSIA 0 (0–0) after extra time. *Mexico*

URUGUAY: Mazurkiewicz; Ubinas, Ancheta, Matosas, Mujica; Maneiro, Cortes, Montero Castillo; Cubilla, Fontes (Gomez), Morales (Esparrago).
RUSSIA: Kavazashvili; Dzodzuashvili, Afonin, Khurtsilava (Logofet), Chesternijev; Muntijan, Asatiani (Kiselev), Kaplichni; Evriuzhkinzin, Bychevetz, Khmelnitzki.
SCORER: Esparrago for Uruguay.

Semi-Finals

ITALY 4, WEST GERMANY 3 (1–0) (1–1) after extra time. *Mexico City*

ITALY: Albertosi; Cera; Burgnich, Bertini, Rosato, (Poletti) Facchetti; Domenghini, Mazzola (Rivera), De Sisti; Boninsegna, Riva.
WEST GERMANY: Maier; Schnellinger; Vogts, Schulz, Beckenbauer, Patzke; Seeler, Overath; Grabowski, Muller, Loehr (Libuda).

SCORERS: Boninsegna, Burgnich, Riva, Rivera, for Italy; Schnellinger, Muller (2) for West Germany.

BRAZIL 3, URUGUAY 1 (1–1). *Guadalajara*

BRAZIL: Felix; Carlos Alberto, Brito, Piazza, Everaldo; Clodoaldo, Gerson; Jairzinho, Tostao, Pelé, Rivelino.
URUGUAY: Mazurkiewicz; Ubinas, Ancheta, Matosas, Mujica; Montero Castillo, Cortes, Fontes; Cubilla, Maneiro (Esparrago), Morales.
SCORERS: Cubilla for Uruguay; Clodoaldo, Jairzinho, Rivelino for Brazil.

Third Place Match

WEST GERMANY 1, URUGUAY 0 (1–0). *Mexico City*

WEST GERMANY: Walter; Schnellinger (Lorenz); Patzke, Fichtel, Weber, Vogts; Seeler, Overath; Libuda (Loehr), Muller, Held.
URUGUAY: Mazurkiewicz; Ubinas, Ancheta, Matosas, Mujica; Montero Castillo, Cortes, Fontes (Sandoval); Cubilla, Maneiro (Esparrago), Morales.
SCORER: Overath for West Germany.

Final

BRAZIL 4, ITALY 1 (1–1). *Mexico City*

BRAZIL: Felix; Carlos Alberto, Brito, Piazza, Everaldo; Clodoaldo, Gerson; Jairzinho, Tostao, Pelé, Rivelino.
ITALY: Albertosi; Cera; Burgnich, Bertini (Juliano), Rosato, Facchetti; Domenghini, Mazzola, De Sisti; Boninsegna (Rivera), Riva.
SCORERS: Pelé, Gerson, Jairzinho, Carlos Alberto for Brazil; Boninsegna for Italy.

3 HOLLAND FINALISTS ON TWO OCCASIONS

Victorious West Germany – at last (1974)

Second in the tournament of 1966; third in that of 1970 West Germany finally got their reward in the 1974 World Cup finals. They had received a fillip two years previously when, with Gunther Netzer at the top of his form as a play-maker in midfield, they had won the 1972 edition of the European Nations Championship; and they had received a recent bit of prompting when a club side, Bayern Munich, had won the 1974 edition of the European Champions' Cup.

For the first time since 1950 the format would be changed with the top two teams in each group not moving on to contest the Quarter-finals but to play in two further groups. The winners of these would contest the Final; the teams who would finish second would meet to decide the third and fourth places.

In 1970 it was teams from the Americas who had won four of the eight places for the Quarter-finals and had provided the most convincing winners of any tournament to date, but four years later the boot was very much on the European foot with West Germany being followed home by Holland and Poland. The Holland of Cruyff, of Neeskens, of Van Hanegem in fact could stand comparison with the most commanding of the sides which had won the World Cup for Brazil. And the measure of the superiority shown by European sides was the fact that the only occasion on which a South American team had a victory over a European one was when Brazil defeated East Germany in a match from the Second Round. In truth the South American sides suffered most terribly from their lack of physical preparation – with Uruguay in particular exercising the most lethal form of thuggery; especially when they met Holland in a game in the First Round.

Brazil opened the tournament by playing very defensively against Yugoslavia. True Pelé had chosen not to play; Gerson, Tostao and Clodoaldo had all suffered vital injuries and the only members of the 1970 side left were Rivelino and Jairzinho but the great strength of the team on this occasion seemed to lie in its defence with Leao proving a more than useful goalkeeper, with Luis Pereira proving an excellent central defender and with the blond fullback, Francisco Marinho, surging forward with some useful runs down the left side of the field: o–o then with the Yugoslavs being impressive in the second part of the game. Maric had shown that he was a fine goalkeeper, Buljan made several telling interceptions at the back and Acimovic had been most intelligent in suggesting pathways for the attack.

Brazil's next game would also be goalless – but on this occasion against Scotland who had beaten Zaire 2–o in their first game in the Group. In the first twenty minutes the champions from South America seemed set to tear Scotland apart with their inventive football and skill at taking free-kicks; but gradually Scotland came into the game strongly and as the game progressed the authority of Billy Bremner in midfield became absolute. David Hay became an increasingly important figure alongside him and both men saw scoring chances pass inches wide on the wrong side of the goalpost. With Holton and Buchan totally neutralising the potential threat from Jairzinho; with Lorimer and Morgan having fine games; with Bremner and Hay sealing up the middle of the field by their intelligent use of the ball – many people thought Scotland were desperately unfortunate not to gain a win. Yugoslavia demolished Zaire 9–o on the same day, so Scotland went into the next game against Yugoslavia needing to win; or hoping against hope that Brazil would win by less than a two-goal margin against Zaire. With the two matches taking place at the same time matters looked promising at half-time, for Brazil had been unable to score more than once; and the Scotland–Yugoslavia game was still goalless. But halfway through the second period a Rivelino left-footed shot screamed into the Zaire goal; and soon after Valdomiro added a third. Worse was to follow as Karasi, who had come on the field only minutes before as a substitute for the Yugo-

slavians, scored with a header which left Scotland needing two
goals in seven minutes. It was not to be, however, for although
Jordan scored in the final minute of the game, Scotland were left
rueing their failure to score against Brazil and the plain truth that
they had taken matters far too easily against Zaire. They would
have the small consolation of remaining the only team playing in
the tournament to stay unbeaten and the fact that Bremner and
McGrain would feature prominently in the lists of the best players
who had been on duty in West Germany.

Group I saw the host nation being drawn against Australia,
Chile and East Germany: the first occasion on which the two
Germanies had played each other since the partition after the last
war. Chile had come to the tournament by a curious route. They
had been forced to play a deciding eliminator against Russia, had
been there and drawn o–o, then had been given a walk-over to the
Finals proper when the Russians had refused to play the return
match in Santiago – a refusal which had much more to do with
political than sporting reasons, since Chile had recently experienced a right-wing coup! Despite some sinuous dribbling on the
part of Caszely, some vigorous defensive work by Figueroa and
some sharp bursts of counter-attacking by Ahumada, the West
Germans hung on to win by just a single goal. Chile next held East
Germany, who had beaten a gallant Australia 2–0, to a 1–1 draw.
In their turn West Germany beat Australia 3–0 which, of course,
meant that when the two Germanies played their 'inaugural'
match the home side were already qualified to play in the Second
Round; so it came as little surprise to find the East defeating the
West merely by the one goal – a defeat which meant that West
Germany would (be able to!) avoid the thrilling Holland team for a
further handful of matches.

In truth Holland had enthralled everybody in their opening
matches. Teams representing Dutch clubs had featured in five of
the previous six editions of the European Cup, and had been
victorious on four occasions; and the coach responsible for the
pressing football that had gained an enormous reputation all over
the world, Rinus Michels, had recently been called back to take
charge of the Holland squad. The team contained exciting full-

backs in Suurbier and Krol, gifted players in the midfield in
Neeskens and Van Hanegem and in attack they possessed in Johan
Cruyff one of the two best players in the tournament (the other
being Franz Beckenbauer). Certainly their class was immediately
apparent in the first game they played, a 2–0 victory against a crude
and ruthless Uruguay. Uruguay played as though they were totally
deprived of skill and talent; three players were cautioned, Julio
Montero Castillo was sent off for aiming a series of knee-high
tackles, and only Mazurkiewicz in goal and Rocha in midfield
showed any type of form. A 1–1 draw against Bulgaria and a 3–0
defeat by Sweden and it was small wonder that Roberto Porta, the
Uruguayan manager, stated just prior to the return of the team to
Montevideo, 'This is the worst football we have ever played. It is a
national disgrace.'

Sweden had proved to be one of the most interesting of teams in
the opening games. They began with two goalless draws against
Bulgaria and Holland but in their 3–0 win over the Uruguayans
they had showed that they were coming into useful form at just the
right time. They possessed one of the better goalkeepers in the
tournament in Ronnie Hellstroem, had useful players in midfield
in Grahn and Bo Larsson and in Edstroem were served by one of
the most skilful of goalscorers. And the two teams to move on to
the Second Round, therefore, were Sweden and Holland, who
slaughtered Bulgaria 4–1 with two of their goals coming from
penalties by Neeskens.

In Group IV we had a riveting start to the second half of the
game between Italy and Haiti when the first goal came from . . .
Haiti! In fact that score by Sanon was the first goal to have been let
in by Dino Zoff for 1,143 minutes of international play. It set the
football world wondering: were we in for as big an upset as
England's defeat in 1950 at the hands of the United States or as
Italy's defeat in 1966 at the hands of North Korea? No. Italy pulled
themselves together and although the goalkeeper for Haiti, Francillon, made a series of superb saves, the Italians ran out 3–1
winners at the end of the game. A sour footnote to this, for a Haiti
defender Ernest Jean-Joseph was found to have taken drugs
before the match, was beaten up and sent home in disgrace on the

orders of Jean-Claude Duvalier, son of 'Papa Doc'. RIP?

On the same day Poland, the conquerors of England in the
qualification group, made their first appearance in the competition
when they faced Argentina – and fascinated everybody with the
poise of their football. Many members of this team had taken part
two years earlier when Poland had been Olympic champions; in
Deyna they had one of the most intelligent and skilful of midfield
players on view; in the young Zmuda and the tall, blond Gorgon
they possessed a pair of effective central defenders; and in Lato
and Szarmach they had players who could score smoothly. In fact
both struck in the 3–2 win by Poland; and these two scored four
goals in the 7–0 triumph over Haiti – with the prowess of
Francillon ensuring that the defeat did not enter double figures as
he made one crucial save after another. It was small wonder that in
the following season he would come to West Germany to play his
football as a mercenary.

On the same day Argentina and Italy played out an entertaining
1–1 draw. Despite the presence of 50,000 Italian supporters in the
crowd of just under 72,000, the Italians just could not put things
right. Although Mazzola played intelligently throughout the game
both Riva and Rivera were badly 'off song'; and a vital mistake on
the part of the Italian coach, Feruccio Valcarreggi, made the game
awkward for Italy when, as a marker for the small, lively, Argentine
winger Houseman, he appointed Capello – an attacking midfield
player! This move turned Capello into a quasi-fullback; and
although Valcarreggi understood his mistake too late, the damage
had already been done. Houseman it was who scored for Argentina; and the only manner in which the Italians could score their
goal (which fortunately for them made the game a draw) was to
force the Argentine centreback, Perfumo, to put the ball into his
own net. So they went into their next game against Poland
requiring just a draw to pass through to the next round.

Alas, it was not to be. Poland won 2–1 but in truth the Italians
were overwhelmed. Mazzola played effectively throughout, Anas-
tasi was incisive in the first-half and Facchetti resolute in the
second, but the Poland midfield of Deyna, Kasperczak and Maszczyk was dominant throughout, with the first-named being the

best player on view as well as the scorer of one of the Polish goals.
With Argentina beating Haiti 4–1, with Babington continuing his
good run of form and despite the heroics of Francillon in the Haiti
goal, the Italians finished third in their qualifying group, behind
Argentina on goal difference. Small wonder that *La Squadra* found
itself being attacked as it left the stadium by its 'supporters'!

East Germany, West Germany, Yugoslavia, Brazil, Holland,
Sweden, Poland and Argentina therefore went through to the
Second Round. Holland, in their first game, set about the unfortunate Argentina in the manner born, with Cruyff scoring once in
each half and with the whole team totally dominating the game.
The other goals in the 4–0 victory came from Rep and Krol and,
although Suurbier was forced to leave the field injured, the Dutch
were extremely fortunate in team selection throughout the championship, having comparatively few injuries, and they were able to
choose ten of their team for all seven of the games.

In the same group Brazil defeated East Germany by just the
single goal. In the 60th minute they were awarded a free-kick some
ten metres outside the East German penalty area, Dirceu broke
from the 'wall' at the last moment and allowed a cannonball of a
shot from Rivelino to scream through. A fast-moving drive from
Rivelino was the first score in their next game against Argentina – a
game which Brazil won by 2–1, and the reply soon after by Brindisi
was the first goal to be given away in the tournament by Brazil. A
header by Jairzinho proved to be the eventual goal, and Brazil
moved on to play the Dutch in their final game in the group; there
they received a nice, sharp lesson in football skill, for although the
introduction of Dirceu on the left side of the midfield had given
them a far greater degree of penetration, they were still a team
lacking in the highest of talents. In the crucial game their defenders chopped and hacked the Dutch from the outset, encouraging
the retribution which their opponents were not slow to deliver. Ze
Maria perpetrated a rugby tackle on Cruyff; Neeskens found
himself being knocked cold by one of the centre-backs in Mario
Marinho then being scythed down by the other, Luis Pereira. For
his pains Pereira found himself being sent off. But the two goals in
the first period of the second-half were worth waiting for: Nees-

kens played a free-kick to Cruyff on his right, dashed forward and
struck the return over the head of the Brazilian goalkeeper, Leao.
And the second was scored by Cruyff driving home a centre by
Rensenbrink. It was a memorable day, indeed, for Dutch football
which had seemed to say 'The King is Dead, Long Live the
King'.

It came as no surprise to learn that the response after the game
in Brazil was severe: coffins of the leading players were paraded in
the streets and an effigy of Zagalo, the manager, was burnt.

The other group saw matches between West Germany and
Yugoslavia, won by the Germans 2–0, and between Poland and
Sweden won by the Poles by just the odd goal, scored by the man
who would finish as the leading scorer in the tournament, Lato. In
the first of these games West Germany for the first time in this
tournament used Rainer Bonhof, whose skills with the ball and
intelligent running into space gave a new dimension to the play of
the European Nations Champions, so that the second half of the
game should have seen more than the second goal scored by Gerd
Muller. And most noticeable in the other game was the dribbling
of Gadocha, the opportunism of Lato, the acrobatics of the
goalkeeper Tomaszewski, and the organisation of Deyna. In fact,
after losing this encounter it fell to the Swedes to tackle West
Germany, a game which they lost 4–2, three of these goals being
scored soon after half-time in a three-minute period.

The fortunes of the two teams were reversed at half-time,
Sweden going in with a 1–0 lead; but West Germany came back
strongly, with Bonhof in particular in glorious form on the right
side of their midfield, scoring the second goal that put his side into
the lead.

On the same day Poland beat Yugoslavia 2–1 with goals from
Deyna and Lato; a score that was repeated three days later when
Sweden beat the Yugoslavs but since neither side could hope to
progress further, this game turned out to be packed with entertaining and spirited football, with both Maric and Hellstroem given
many opportunities to show what excellent goalkeepers they were.
(Indeed, many thought that they were the two most gifted goalkeepers in the entire tournament.) And this left the match between

West Germany and Poland to decide which team would take part in the final.

West Germany won by a second-half goal by Gerd Muller, but many felt that the game should not have taken place when it did. A rainstorm had made the pitch unplayable, and although the West German authorities drew off as much water as they could and put the time of the match back, it could have been postponed until the following day. Tomaszewski saved a penalty from Holzenbein, but in the first-half Maier made an incredible double-save from Lato and Gadocha to put heart into the Germans. Beckenbauer was beginning to display authoritative form in defence, and the midfield of Bonhof, Hoeness and Overath gradually stood up to the Polish wiles of Deyna and Kaspercak.

Poland would have the small satisfaction of beating Brazil in the match to determine third and fourth places: a just reward for having entertained so many people with their thrilling football over the previous four weeks. The goal was from Lato, Poland showing itself once more to be thoroughly more imaginative and interesting; Brazil had a strong defence and midfield but a pitifully inadequate attack. It was an uninspiring game.

But the Final, the following day, got off to an electric start when Holland were awarded a penalty by the English referee, Jack Taylor, within the first minute and before any West German had touched the ball! 1–0 to Holland, and for the following twenty-five minutes the Dutch arrogantly rolled the ball about to each other, making pretty patterns, and under no threat whatsoever from the West Germans, who were entirely stunned. Then West Germany were awarded a penalty of their own when Holzenbein was tripped inside the area by Jansen, and when Gerd Muller gave West Germany a 2–1 lead just before half-time the Dutch were really shaken. The crucial issue in the match, however, was the man-to-man marking of Cruyff by the West German fullback, Bertie Vogts. Cruyff was undoubtedly the most gifted attacking player in the tournament, possessing a footballing brain that was lightning fast, and all the attributes of phenomenal players – lovely balance, glorious ball control and an exceptional shot in either foot. With his being so effectively shackled throughout the game, the effect on Holland, in psychological as well as in physical terms, was crucial; and after the West Germans had been awarded a penalty they played with new spirit, Franz Beckenbauer very astutely marshalling his forces in defence. With Rainer Bonhof spurring the midfield, and Grabowski aiding Muller up front, West Germany were able to hang on to that first-half lead and take the tenth edition of the World Cup.

It had been a real mixture of a tournament. Among the matters that had been frowned upon some said that the new formula for the tournament had led to much careless or plain bad football which had seen the eventual champions beaten in an unimportant game from the First Round. But surely no game should be described as being 'unimportant'? And then there had been the fact that while Australia had battled bravely the other two weaker teams, Zaire and Haiti, had conceded 28 goals between them. Elementary arithmetic, here, for without those games and goals you get 69 goals in 32 games which would be by some measure the worst goals per game average. In addition some nations – or rather the players of some nations – had taken to demanding fees for giving interviews and vast sums for succeeding in winning the title.

On the positive side, however, was the firmness and quality of some of the refereeing and many, many moments of memorable footballing skills. If the West German team that had won the European Nations Championship two years previously had played more fluid and imaginative football than the new holders of the World Cup, some of the most memorable football had been played by Sweden, by Poland and by Holland. Especially Holland, who would be in the forefront of the competition four years later.

1974 – Final Stages

Group A

	P	W	D	L	F	A	Pts
HOLLAND	3	3	0	0	8	0	6
BRAZIL	3	2	0	1	3	3	4
EAST GERMANY	3	0	1	2	1	4	1
ARGENTINA	3	0	1	2	2	7	1

Group B

	P	W	D	L	F	A	Pts
WEST GERMANY	3	3	0	0	7	2	6
POLAND	3	2	0	1	3	2	4
SWEDEN	3	1	0	2	4	6	2
YUGOSLAVIA	3	0	0	3	2	6	0

Third Place Match played in Munich

POLAND 1, BRAZIL 0 (1–0) Lato for Poland

POLAND: Tomaszewski; Szymanowski, Gorgon, Musial; Kasperc-
zak (Cmikiewicz), Deyna, Maszczyk; Lato, Szarmach (Kapka),
Gadocha.
BRAZIL: Leao; Ze Maria, Alfredo, M. Marinho, F. Marinho; Paulo
Cesar Carpeggiani, Rivelino, Ademir da Guia (Mirandinha);
Valdomiro, Jairzinho, Dirceu.

Final played in Munich

WEST GERMANY 2, HOLLAND 1 (2–1) Breitner (pen.),
Muller for West Germany and Neeskens (pen.) for Holland

WEST GERMANY: Maier; Vogts, Schwarzenbeck, Beckenbauer,
Breitner; Bonhof, Hoeness, Overath; Grabowski, Muller, Hol-
zenbein.
HOLLAND: Jongbloed; Suurbier, Rijsbergen (De Jong), Haan,
Krol; Jansen, Neeskens, Van Hanegem; Rep, Cruyff, Rensen-
brink (R. Van de Kerkhof).

Another Home Victory in Argentina (1978)

Never has a political background so affected a World Cup tournament. Before the military junta of General George Videla seized
power in 1976, many had been extremely concerned that the 1978
edition of the World Cup had been given to Argentina; but after
the coup fears were increased when thousands of people were
tortured, imprisoned without trial or simply 'disappeared', never
to be heard of again. The junta set up a new body, the Ente
Autarquico Mundial to make sure that all preparations for the
tournament – including the construction of three new stadia and
the remodelling of three others – would be carried out in time.
And there can be little doubt that, without the setting up of the
EAM and the hard work done by this body, the tournament would
probably have been relocated to Brazil, Mexico or Spain. And the
corollary of that, of course, was that there was that much more
extra pressure on Argentina to win!

The presence of great players obviously helps the prestige of a
tournament: and, sadly, the two heroes of the 1974 World Cup
chose not to take part. Franz Beckenbauer had, fifteen months
previously, signed for New York Cosmos for $2,500,000 and

Johan Cruyff absolutely refused to take part, despite huge offers.
These two were not the only absentees. West Germany had to
compete without the talents of Gerd Muller, Wolfgang Overath,
Paul Breitner, Uli Hoeness and Jurgen Grabowski; and Wim van
Hanegem dropped out at the last moment after being informed
that he could not count on a regular place in the side. The host
country, Argentina, had lost several players from her 1974 side
who had moved to play in Europe such as Kempes, Brindisi,
Carnevali, Wolff and Heredia, who were now in Spain, and
Babington who had moved to West Germany. When it came down
to it Cesar-Luis Menotti, nick-named El Flaco (the Thin One)
expressed interest in only Kempes, Wolff and Oswaldo Piazza
playing at centre-back for the French club of St Etienne. In the
event, Wolff could not be released by Real Madrid and the family
of Piazza were involved in a road accident, so Kempes was the only
man to join the squad.

Scotland were favoured by many. They had had a successful
tour of South America in 1977, and in their qualifying group had
eliminated the 1976 winners of the European Championship,
Czechoslovakia. Even though their final win in the qualifying
round had been in part thanks to a penalty that wasn't in their
match away against Wales, euphoria was high. WE'RE ON OUR
WAY TO RIO trumpeted a headline in a Scottish daily paper
with a neat disregard for geography. 'Of course we'll win the
World Cup. If I say that it saves you from asking me again,' said the
ebullient Scottish manager Ally Macleod, who favoured Hungary
were Scotland not to succeed in their mission! (Hungary joined
Mexico as being the only two countries not to win any point
whatsoever.) He paid a visit to Cordoba in the January of 1978 and
was delighted with the accommodation – so the feedback to
Scotland's fans was just what they required. But the few realists in
their camp had other evidence. Danny McGrain would be ruled
out of this World Cup through injury; Gordon McQueen, the
first-choice stopper, would receive an injury only a fortnight
before the tournament that would rule him out; and much to the
surprise of everyone, Andy Gray, the young central striker who
was on top form, would not make the selection.

Brazil were favourites to do well, perhaps even to win the tournament. They had dismissed Oswaldo Brandao a year previously and had appointed in his place a young army captain, Claudio Coutinho, who was attempting to 'Europeanise' the Brazilian game by placing the emphasis on stamina and covering each blade of grass on the pitch. A far cry indeed from those days of Pelé, Gerson and Tostao. Coutinho had compounded his strategy by not selecting Francisco Marinho, who had been one of the most-admired fullbacks in the previous tournament as well as that wayward forward, Paulo Cesar.*

Italy, the conquerors of the qualifying group above England – and the only team to qualify on goal difference – were given scant chance of success. The chief play-maker to the team, Giancarlo Antognoni, had been having a desperate season trying to prevent his club side of Fiorentia from being relegated; and for some months had suffered a strain to his right ankle which had required a complete rest. In addition, his wife had a miscarriage only a few days prior to Italy's first game against France. Giacinto Facchetti, the sweeper, was ruled out of football altogether, having been on the receiving end of a tackle from Romeo Benetti. The team had recently recruited a young fullback, Cabrini, who was strong in the tackle and eager to set up counter-attacks; at their training camp, spent just outside Buenos Aires, Enzo Bearzot, the Italian manager, decided that the time had come to be brave and to play Paolo Rossi the young, adroit and courageous forward who had just finished the season in Italy as the chief scorer. With Marco Tardelli settling firmly into his role as a defensive player in midfield Bearzot hoped, above all, to encourage the Italian team to play more open football, completely throw off those defensive shackles which were set firm in the Italian club game and attempt to play more freely. He would have his wish much sooner than he could have expected!

It came after thirty-eight seconds of play in the first of Italy's

* Soon after the finish of the tournament Coutinho was to drown in an accident at sea.

games in Group I when Didier Six collected a glorious through
pass from the midfield, raced down the left touchline and crossed
the ball into the centre for Bernard Lacombe to out-jump the
Italian defence and head a simple goal. Thunder-struck the
Italians simply knew that they had then to attack and take the game
into the French half, to stand any chance of gaining a victory and
driven on by the experience of Romeo Benetti, by the fact that
Tardelli carried out a masterly shackling job on Michel Platini, by
the smooth manner in which Bettega and Rossi formed a part-
nership in the attack, Italy won the game 2–1. On the same day
Argentina had had a 2–1 win over Hungary with two Hungarians,
Nyilasi and Toroscik, being sent off for committing ugly fouls at
the end of the game. Yet the atmosphere in the River Plate stadium
was sour from the start, with a snowstorm of Argentinian favours
thrown onto the pitch as the teams came out; tension throughout
that could have been cut with a knife.

Four days later Italy had little difficulty in defeating a depleted
Hungarian team 3–1 but one of the best matches of the tournament was to take place that same evening in Buenos Aires when
Argentina defeated a gallant France by a 2–1 scoreline. It was truly
an enthralling spectacle, every minute packed with good football –
and atrocious refereeing decisions on the part of the Swiss
officials; Jean Dubach, 'gave' Argentina a penalty when the
accomplished black sweeper Marius Tresor landed on the ball
while challenging Luque in the penalty area and was adjudged to
have handled it intentionally. And this in injury time! It was a
monstrous decision compounding the fact that the referee had
failed to award France a penalty of their own when Six was pulled
down in the penalty area. And the same player should have scored,
following a glorious run by Platini, but shot wide when he had only
the goalkeeper to beat. Lucky, lucky Argentina.

Thus when Argentina met Italy again (following their drawn
game in the 1974 tournament) both sides had already qualified for
the Second Round. The match was, however, still important, as
Argentina very much wished to stay in Buenos Aires and not have
to travel to Rosario, over 300 kilometres to the north-east of the
capital: which would be their fate if they failed to secure a victory.

There would be no nonsense on this occasion about the refereeing
for the choice had fallen to Abraham Klein who made it clear from
the first that he would not 'play the gallery'. With the Italians
knowing that a draw would suit them – falling back on defensive
man-to-man marking and making sudden breaks from defence
into attack – the only goal of the game came in the sixty-seventh
minute when, after an interchange of passes between Antognoni
and Rossi, the latter slid a perfectly placed pass through to Bettega,
who screwed his shot past Fillol, the commanding goalkeeper for
Argentina. But although it was Bettega who won most of the glory,
it should be pointed out that both Benetti and Causio ran their
hearts out in midfield, and Gentile (called in as stopper after
Cuccureddu had replaced the injured Bellugi) completely marked
Kempes out of the game. And in the afternoon of the same day
France received some reward when they defeated Hungary 3–1. A
curious event happened before the game when France were asked
to change their strip because television viewers with black and
white sets found it hard to differentiate between the blue of France
and the red of Hungary. A sure sign, this, of interests other than
simple footballing ones being considered! Even though France
were forced to leave the tournament after this wi.i, they made a
tournament record that year by being the only country playing to
have used all twenty-two of their permitted players, with Marius
Tresor the only man to have played in all 270 minutes of their
games.

Group II saw West Germany play Poland play Mexico play
Tunisia: the easiest of all the four groups. Sadly, it got off to a
goalless draw between West Germany and Poland – the fourth
occasion in succession that the opening game in the tournament
has been something of a 'goalless grimmie'. Deyna was the man of
the match directing operations in the midfield with skill and
intelligence, and several famous faces from the Polish triumph of
four years earlier were there: Gorgon and Zmuda in the middle of
the defence and Lato and Szarmach in the attack. Also there was
Wlodzimierz Lubanski, who had been put out of the game entirely
for two years with an injury he had received in June 1973 when
England had played Poland in Warsaw. Was this draw inevitable?

Many people thought so, with both teams ensuring a place for
themselves in the last eight.

The following day Tunisia amazed many people by defeating
Mexico 3–1. Like many of the unknown teams in the past they
possessed a player of absolute class, a slim character in their
midfield, Dhiab Tarak, who laid on all three goals for the African
side – all scored in the second half, after Mexico had scored from a
penalty just before half-time. This was a real test of character, and
the group table at the end of the day would show Tunisia standing
proudly above West Germany, Poland, and Mexico who had put
on a pathetic display. Four days later Tunisia proved their worth
against an altogether stronger team by holding Poland to a 1–0
win, totally dominating the second half and being most unfortunate not to gain a draw. Meanwhile Mexico was proving itself the
weakest team in the competition by losing 6–0 to West Germany.
And as if to add insult to injury, Tunisia next held West Germany
to a goalless draw while Poland beat Mexico 3–1, although
Tomaszewski in their goal was called upon to save some five close
shots from his opponents.

If the real heroes of the first two groups had been teams which
would take no further part in the competition the games from the
third group seemed more concerned with watching Brazil – the
9–4 favourites before the competition started – try to beat itself
and not qualify for the Second Round. It was an unhappy ship.
Rivelino was overweight and rebellious; Coutinho had fallen out
with Zico, another of the stars; and it was as well that Amaral and
Oscar played magnificently at the heart of the defence so that
Brazil were the only team playing in this tournament to remain
unbeaten, and that Batista and Cerezo produced play of the first
order in midfield. They were held to a 1–1 draw by Sweden in the
opening game; and then drew 0–0 with Spain in the game which
they surely would have lost had not Cardenosa missed a marvellous chance when right in front of the goal. In their third game,
however, they beat Austria 1–0. But Austria had already qualified,
thanks to two wins against Spain (2–1) and Sweden (1–0) which
left these two to play each other and see which team would go
through if Brazil slipped up. Spain won this affair 1–0 – but they

must have been somewhat forlorn to leave the competition after having showed the most marvellous spirit in defeating Rumania and Yugoslavia in their qualifying games.

Group IV saw Scotland drawn against Iran, Peru and Holland; a draw which Ally Macleod, the Scottish manager, said he 'wanted'. 'That leaves us to go through to the last eight with Holland and after that the players won't need any motivating.' We were never to find out, because although Scotland took an early lead against Peru and completely dominated the first period of the first half, things began to go sadly wrong. Cubillas, Munante and Oblitas at last decided to run at the Scottish defence and gradually started to drive it wild with a succession of one-twos. Finally, the inevitable happened, and in the forty-second minute Peru finally scored through Cueto. A disastrous moment at which to give away a goal. Worse was to follow, however, in the sixty-fourth minute, when Scotland were awarded a penalty after Rioch was brought down by Cubillas. Masson took the kick but it was a truly feeble effort which Quiroga, in the Peruvian goal, found no trouble in saving. That was Scotland's last chance, for Peru totally dominated the last 25 minutes of the game. Cubillas scored twice – and Scotland had a bitter postscript when Willie Johnston their wing-forward, was found to have taken 'pep' pills. So morale for the next match, against Iran, couldn't have been lower.

Maybe that excuse could be used profitably, because the match was one of the very worst there has ever been in the history of the World Cup. Surely Scotland have never played such bad football? The result was a 1–1 draw, with Scotland's score coming from an own goal by Eskandarjan; one of the best Scottish players Martin Buchan was kicked in the face by the man whose role at fullback he had taken in the first match, Willie Donachie; and it could so easily have been another traumatic defeat had not Ghasimpour shot straight at Rough when put through in the first half. No wonder the hundreds of Scottish supporters, who had travelled over 9,000 kilometres to Argentina, began to wail with fury; no wonder that restaurants in Glasgow which in former times had used the name of the Scotland manager in their advertising started to put up signs which read, 'Ally MacLeod does NOT eat here'!

Holland had shown how it could be done by beating Iran 3–0 and when it became the turn of Peru they won 4–1; so when these two sides met it came as no surprise to find them playing very cagily, settling for a 0–0 draw.

Experts often point out that Scotland play terribly against poor teams, handsomely against the good ones. And so it proved when Scotland played Holland in their final match. The team selection was put right at long last, with Souness being played in midfield and proving that he was exactly the right link to get the best out of Dalglish up front. In fact it was Dalglish who volleyed Scotland's equaliser ten minutes after Rensenbrink had given Holland a lead in the thirty-fourth minute with a penalty: the thousandth goal in the history of the World Cup. Scotland got their retribution early in the second half when Gemmill scored a penalty after Krol was adjudged to have fouled Souness, and in the sixty-eighth minute the same player scored what was admitted by some to be the best goal of this World Cup, when he jinked his way through the Dutch defence to score with a hard shot from close range. The Scottish supporters had a bare four minutes of wishful thinking about their appearance in the Second Round before Rep laid their wish to rest, scoring with a screaming shot from 23 metres.

What had gone wrong with Scotland and their hopes? Partly the blame lay in the arrogance with which Scotland had gone to Argentina, having done far too little homework as to the strengths and weaknesses of their opponents; partly it lay in team selection – in the loyalty to Rioch and Masson, who had been dropped by their club sides, in the under-use of Souness; partly it lay in the accommodation which left the players very bored when not depressed; and partly with the players themselves – many of whom simply did not realise how much they had let down their supporters. But these supporters themselves were to blame. 'Bring on the English' they roared when, at one stage in the game against Holland, they seemed to be in with a chance of reaching the last eight.

Group A in the Second Round consisted of Italy, West Germany, Austria and Holland; Group B of Argentina, Poland, Brazil and Peru. Of these, Italy was the only country to have won all its

games in the early stages and those wins had been achieved in what
many people thought had been the most difficult group, and by a
new formula of play: Enzo Bearzot had dragged his players away
from the negativity induced by *catenaccio* (man-to-man marking
plus a sweeper) and introducing the Total Football which had
been played by Holland in the previous World Cup and the West
German team in 1972.

In their first game in the Second Round Italy played West
Germany, and optimists hoped for an encounter as entertaining as
that when they had last met in a World Cup, the 4–3 victory by Italy
in a Semi-final in 1970. No chance of that on this occasion: Italy
were now regarded as an attacking team and from the first moment
West Germany settled down to play a form of *catenaccio* with
Rumenigge and Holzenbein on the wings being drawn back to play
in midfield and Klaus Fischer left alone in the attack. 0–0 the
result (the third goalless draw out of West Germany's four games
to date), but Bettega missed two chances from close distance – and
the Italian triumphal march had been stopped.

On the same day Holland had a most uplifting 5–1 victory over
Austria in Cordoba. The Dutch players showed fresh zest on
being away at last from the heights of Mendoza; Holland were able
to call upon some talented substitutes in Pieter Wildschut and
Erny Brandts, the 22-year-old centre-back; and the injury to
Neeskens had given a chance to Arie Haan. Johnny Rep scored
two of the goals and Robbie Rensenbrink scored from a penalty
and showed that he was coming back into form. A most significant
win, this, in psychological terms, as well as being most disheartening
for the other teams.

Four days later Holland played West Germany at Cordoba, with
the Dutch hyper-keen to reverse the result of the previous World
Cup Final. They began their mission miserably, going down after
only three minutes to a tap-in by Abramczik, when a thundering
free-kick by Bonhof had only been parried by Schrivers, but when
they equalised in the twenty-sixth minute it was with a truly
memorable shot on the part of Haan, who let fly from roughly 25
metres out. Maier never even touched the ball. It was the first
occasion in which he had been beaten in 475 minutes of play in

World Cup games: a new record. West Germany, however, were playing with considerably more character than they had shown in their game against Italy, and took the lead again in the seventieth minute when Dieter Muller headed in a centre; it was only after Holland had taken off Wildschut and substituted that angular forward, Dirk Nanninga, that they were able to get a draw from the game. He it was who helped Rene Van der Kerkhof slice in from the left and put the ball past Maier from a narrow distance.

On the same day in Buenos Aires Italy beat Austria 1–0, thanks to a goal from Rossi scored in the thirteenth minute – after which the team just fell back on defence. Austria showed very little wit or imagination in their play (in fact that goal of Rossi's had followed an unwise back pass from a fullback), and Krankl spent much of the game being the lone ranger of the attack. He it was who scored the decisive goal three days later when Austria beat West Germany 3–2 after volleying the Austrian second goal. A very sad way for Helmut Schön to retire as manager of the West German team: first, third and second in the preceeding editions of the tournament. On the same day Holland came to play Italy in Buenos Aires. Thanks to their 5–1 victory over Austria they knew that all they had to do was to gain a draw. But in the first ten minutes Italy could have scored twice, and in fact they took the lead in the nineteenth minute when Brandts skimmed the ball past Schrivers into the goal – in an attempt to stop Bettega from scoring. As well as giving away an own goal, he damaged the right knee of the goalkeeper, who had to be substituted soon after by Jan Jongbloed, the goalkeeper from the 1974 side who, while still 'cold' made two astonishing saves from Rossi and Benetti. Then the wrestling began: Benetti kicked Haan and fouled Rensenbrink, and in retribution Haan booted Zaccarelli and Rep flattened Benetti. By half-time the names of Rep and Benetti were in the book and it was then that Bearzot made the grave mistake of taking off Franco Causio – who had played skilfully down the right wing – and putting on Claudio Sala. The Italian rhythm went and soon after Brandts atoned for his own goal by swinging his right-foot at the ball while surrounded by Italian players and driving the ball through to score; and in the seventy-seventh minute there came once more one of those thunderous shots from Haan from 32 metres out, which nearly removed the back of the net. Two minutes later Italy substituted Graziani for Benetti in an attempt to score twice in the remaining minutes of the game, but to no avail; and the cruel spate of fouling continued with Haan himself and Cabrini and Tardelli being booked. Holland were through to the Final.

In Group B Brazil at last began to play in the manner hoped for by all their supporters. Away from the difficult playing surface at Mar Del Plata, their first match was at Mendoza, where they beat Peru 3–0 thanks to two goals from Dirceu, one of these being from a free kick which swung inwards at the last moment to leave Quiroga toally helpless. Zico came on as substitute in the seventieth minute and scored from a penalty soon after.

That evening Argentina beat Poland 2–0, thanks largely to a skilful display by Mario Kempès who scored both goals in the fifteenth and seventieth minutes, and rescued another by making a spectacular save off the goal-line after Fillol had been beaten. The penalty was taken by Deyna playing in his hundredth international, but his weak shot was saved – and Poland's last chance went. Although in the first half they had played very well, with Boniek and Adam Nawalka outstanding and although a shot from Lato hit the side-netting early in the second half, it became increasingly one-way traffic, with Argentina spurred on by the baying of the crowds, who seemed much more intense at Rosario than they had been in the larger stadium at Buenos Aires. A real 'pressure-cooker' of a ground.

You think that games between England and Scotland have an electric atmosphere? Forget it. When Argentina play Brazil hatred is a factor that is present even before the ball has been kicked. Four players were booked; others 'left their feet' in many instances showing their studs and Ricardo Villa, who had come on for Ardiles after half-time, was extremely fortunate not to be sent off after committing an over-the-ball foul on Batista, the Brazilian midfield player. It was a truly forgettable goalless draw with little football managing to survive all the spitefulness.

In the afternoon of the same day Poland had beaten Peru 1–0

but truly the score could have been in double figures. Why wasn't it? Thanks to that remarkable goalkeeper, Ramon Quiroga, who made amazing saves all through the game and in the final minutes advanced beyond the halfway line in order to break up the Polish attacks. Truly he deserved the nickname of 'El Loco'! The goal for Poland was scored by Szarmach, the woodwork was hit on two occasions and this feeble effort on the part of Peru can only have served to make all Scotsmen round the world feel most distressed by the memory of Scotland's weak displays.

The final day of this Round saw Brazil beat Poland 3–1. But rather it might be put the other way round because the Polish finishing was truly terrible. Both Lato and Szarmach seemed to have lost that vital edge of speed and thought which had made them so successful four years earlier, and although Leao was at the top of his form it is true to say that he absolutely had to be, because Poland's midfield players played with great authority. The first of Brazil's goals came from a swerving free kick of great power struck by Nelinho and the other two from Roberto. In that evening Argentina beat Peru. Why was the game started three-quarters of an hour after the game between Brazil and Poland had actually finished? Because of 'home' advantage; the argument being that Argentina should play all their games in the evening so that the crowds could attend without disrupting their work. Ridiculous. Be that as it may, Argentina knew that the game had to be won by a clear four goals in order to give her a place in the Final. People will always see this game as being a 'fix', but the fact is that poor Peru were just overrun in the second half, after going in 2–0 down at half-time. In fact they could have scored twice themselves in the first half, when Munante and Oblitas both went near with chances. Kempes and Luque scored twice, with the other goals being scored by Tarantini and Houseman (a much less effective player than he had been in 1974). So it was Argentina versus Holland in the Final.

The day before we saw the match between Brazil and Italy to decide third and fourth places. Both teams possessed supporters and experts who thought that they were the best teams in the competition. Brazil had yet to lose a game, while the Italians, in addition to having beaten Argentina, felt that they had played the best football of the tournament. But, as against Holland, Italy allowed itself to be overtaken after Causio had scored a goal in the thirty-eighth minute. First Nelinho shot powerfully from the right corner and the ball swerved *inwards* to defeat Zoff, and the winning goal came from Dirceu, who swung in a fierce shot from just outside the penalty area. So Brazil retained their record of remaining unbeaten; however they could be considered unfortunate in TWO respects at least – that of playing their first round matches at Mar Del Plata on pitches that cut up horribly and of having Argentina play their last game after their own had finished.

Nor did it stop there, for before the Final had begun Holland's players came out onto the field five minutes before the home team, who instantly added to that piece of gamesmanship by objecting to the cast that was being worn by Rene Van der Kerkhof on his right wrist. He had suffered the injury in the first game of the tournament but none of the succeeding five opponents of the Dutch had objected! Eventually he was allowed to keep it on with a covering of bandage, but the psychological damage had been done. It was small wonder Holland began to play in a distressed and ugly mood. In addition, they had two further causes for worry: some most feeble refereeing by Sergio Gonella and the fact that Mario Kempès was in the most splendid form. For a long period the Argentina defence made mistake after mistake with Fillol making two superb saves from Rep and Rensenbrink and then suddenly, in the thirty-seventh minute, Argentina took the lead: Ardiles to Luque to Kempès who slid the ball into the goal, underneath the advancing Jongbloed.

In the first period of the second half each side made two substitutions: Nanninga for Rep, Larrosa for Ardiles, Suurbier for Jansen and Houseman for Ortiz. And it was the first-named of these who headed in a centre from the right in the eighty-first minute. Holland pressed forward even more aggressively and in the eighty-ninth minute Rensenbrink hit a post. Extra time, therefore; the first occasion in a Final since 1966 when another host country, England, had beaten the redoubtable West Germans. And it was during this period when Mario Kempès really came into his own, playing with all the skill, all the speed and all the composure that he knew. Bertoni put him through to score the goal that made him the highest scorer in the competition (although he hadn't scored at all in the first round): in the hundred-and-fourth minute when he struck in a rebound from his original shot; and ten minutes later he was able to play a one-two with Bertoni after which the winger scored. The host team had won for the second time in succession and Holland had had the chagrin of twice being defeated finalists.

102 goals had been scored, much good and entertaining football had been played; there had been thunderous goals from Haan, Rep, Cubillas and Luque, and clever ones from Dirceu, Gemmill, Schachner; there had been much intelligent running with the ball; a fair proportion of the refereeing had been wayward or weak and there had been some incredibly poor decisions – decisions which could have caused changes in some results. But overall the tournament was immensely better than one had dared to hope for and if the number of outstanding individuals was diminished then the mannner in which teamwork had improved since the last tournament was most marked.

The final word, however, must be cautionary. Pressures' on teams and their managers were far too intense and, with the idea of playing the first section of games in groups, we have the situation in which both the last two winners of the tournament had been beaten before they ever reached the Final (West Germany by East Germany in 1974 and Argentina by Italy in 1978). With the next tournament being expanded to include 24 teams, the number of unimportant matches, the amount of bad and boring football, and mistakes by referees was bound to rise, and all the prestige of the World Cup sharply fall.

1978 Final Stages

Group A

HOLLAND	3	2	1	0	9	4	5
ITALY	3	1	1	1	2	2	3
WEST GERMANY	3	0	2	1	4	5	2
AUSTRIA	3	1	0	2	4	8	2

Group B

ARGENTINA	3	2	1	0	8	0	5
BRAZIL	3	2	1	0	6	1	5
POLAND	3	1	0	2	2	5	2
PERU	3	0	0	3	0	10	0

Third Place Match played in Buenos Aires

BRAZIL 2, ITALY 1 (0–1) Nelinho, Dirceu for Brazil, Causio for
Italy

BRAZIL: Leao; Nelinho, Oscar, Amaral, Neto; Cerezo (Rivelino),
Batista, Dirceu; Gil (Reinaldo), Mendonca, Roberto
ITALY: Zoff; Cuccureddu, Gentile, Scirea, Cabrini; Maldera,
Antognoni (Sala C.), Sala P.; Causio, Rossi, Bettega

Final played in Buenos Aires

ARGENTINA 3, HOLLAND 1 (1–0) (1–1) Kempès (2), Bertoni
for Argentina, Nanninga for Holland

ARGENTINA: Fillol; Olguin, Galvan, Passarella, Tarantini; Ardiles
(Darrosa), Gallego, Kempès; Bertoni, Luque, Ortiz (Houseman)
HOLLAND: Jongbloed; Poortvliet, Brandts, Krol, Jansen (Suur-
bier); Haan, Neeskens, Van der Kerkhof W.; Rep (Nanninga),
Rensenbrink, Van der Kerkhof R.

4 ITALY TRIUMPH FOR THE THIRD TIME

The 1982 edition of the World Cup, as forecast by many, proved to be far too cumbersome for its own good. Compared with the original edition, held in Uruguay in 1930 (which had seen 18 matches played in 17 days), it was positively elephantine, providing a total of 52 matches in a period of 28 days. The fact that the number of countries permitted to take part in the Finals had risen to 24 – for the first time – of course ensured that many of the games played were comparatively meaningless since the knock-out principle applied to only the last four matches. Equally negative was the fact that the number of rest days was too few, causing the Semi-final between France and West Germany to be decided by a penalty shoot-out: the first occasion on which this controversial practice had been used to decide a match in the World Cup. Much more fair, surely, to have the match replayed. But no – providing yet another example of the manner in which the game of football had been hijacked by the television and the promotions people so that the rights of the players often seemed to be of secondary importance.

Time and again this could be the only conclusion. Several matches were played in the most appalling heat (the Northern Ireland match against Austria took place in temperature which rose to 45 degrees in Centigrade); the players of France were forced to sit exhausted on their suitcases and watch while plane after plane took off from Seville airport after their Semi-final match against West Germany (small wonder that when it came to the play-off for the Third place the French team was much depleted) and throughout the competition came ceaseless complaints concerning the manner in which the common dignities of the players were being abused by the authorities.

There was no outstanding favourite for the tournament. Brazil were tipped by many and, indeed, possessed a wealth of talent in midfield. Cerezo, Socrates and Zico had provided Brazilian sup-

porters with many moments of magic during the previous two
years and to these had been added Falcao, known as 'Il Divino',
who had been triumphing in Italy during the same period. He was
especially eager to make a point since in 1978 he had been
astonishingly omitted from the Brazilian party. The 1982 side,
however, possessed another in that long line of forgettable goalkeepers in Waldir Peres and caused its supporters no end of
torment by having a defence that was prone to lose concentration.

Argentina's hopes had been high at the start of the year. Many
members of the successful side of four years previously were still
available including the chief scorer, Mario Kempès, who had
experienced success in Spain ever since 1976. If Cesar-Luis
Menotti was still the manager, the authoritative Daniel Passarella
was still in charge of the team on the pitch, and on this occasion it
had another arrow in its quiver – Diego Maradona, a thick-thighed
21-year-old who was being hailed as the most outstanding player
in the world. On March 31, however, General Galtieri decided to
reclaim the Falkland Islands (or Las Malvinas as they are known in
Argentina) by force – and there is no telling the emotive effect that
living through reports of the war meant on the Argentine players,
more than one of whom lost relatives or friends in the fighting.

Of the previous winners of the tournament that came from
Europe, England were mightily fortunate to be competing in the
Final stages at all – and this only after Rumania had amazingly lost
1–2 at home to Switzerland in a match from the Qualifying
tournament. However, after Don Howe (who represented England as right-back in the 1958 tournament) was called in to
organise the defence, England started to look more the part and in
Bryan Robson possessed undoubtedly one of the most gifted
midfield players in the world. West Germany, as so often, seemed
to be a most solid side. The gigantic Horst Hrubesch, who had
been outstanding during the 1980 European Nations Championship, was vying for a place; Karl-Heinz Rummenigge had
been performing so splendidly for his club side of Bayern Munich
that he had been elected European Footballer of the Year for the
second successive time, and there was a thrilling newcomer in
Pierre Littbarski who was as slippery as an eel and possessed a

venomous shot. If there was disappointment that Bernd Schuster
had been ruled out by injury while playing for his club side, FC
Barcelona, this was mitigated by the fact that two other members
of the team possessed vast experience of Spanish footballing
conditions: Paul Breitner having performed recently in midfield
for Real Madrid, the club which currently had on its books his
compatriot, Uli Stielike, the West German sweeper.

The third of these former champions, Italy, entered the tournament in a most pessimistic state. Paolo Rossi had just 'emerged'
from a two-year ban for having been involved in a bribery scandal,
and drastically lacked match fitness. One of the heroes of four
years previously, Roberto Bettega, had failed to recover from a
cruel injury received in a European Cup game during October
while another of their stars, the highly-talented midfielder, Giancarlo Antognoni, had just resumed playing after having received a
near-fatal head wound in a club game at the end of November. Not
surprisingly, Italy had lost recently against both France and East
Germany and had been thankful to gain a draw with Switzerland.
The portents seemed ominous. There is no job in football which
equals the pressures placed upon the shoulders of the Italian
manager, and the likeable Enzo Bearzot found himself on the
receiving end of advice that arrived daily in the Italian sporting
press and which eventually became so sour that the players ceased
to give interviews.

Last of those teams that might have anticipated victory in this
edition of the tournament came the host country, Spain. However,
it had presented a most modest showing at the 1980 European
Nations Championship and the results since had been very mixed.
On that occasion the team had been managed by the brilliant
ex-Hungarian inside-forward, Ladislao Kubala, and had been
inspired from midfield by the Real Sociedad driving-force, Jesus
Zamora. Now the former had been replaced by the former
Uruguayan centre-back, Jose Santamaria, and the latter was
disastrously out-of-form. A third consecutive victory by a side
playing at home seemed, therefore, to be a remote possibility.

These six seeded countries had the immense advantage of being
able to play all their matches in a specific city and were not

required to travel, which could be a most gruelling task. Italy were allotted to Vigo on the western coast of Spain while on the northern and cooler coast West Germany were bound to Gijon and England to Bilbao. All games from these groups in the First Round took place, however, in the late afternoon while evening games were played by teams in the other three groups – Argentina being based in Barcelona, Spain in Valencia and the favourites, Brazil, in Seville.

Possible victors among sides outside this privileged sextet were not many. The Soviet Union had among its forwards the legendary Oleg Blokhin, an authoritative sweeper in Alexandr Chivadze and a highly-acclaimed young goalkeeper in Renat Dassaev but since injury had robbed them of the authority and flair of David Kipiani in the midfield the team lacked a play-maker of quality. Poland had one of the outstanding individuals from four years previously, Zbigniew Boniek, and Wladyslaw Zmuda was still an imposing figure in the centre of the defence, but the team seemed to be short of players of real quality. Belgium had never found a successor for Wilfred Van Moer who by now was in his thirty-seventh year and France, while it had a gloriously-gifted midfield marshalled by Michel Platini and the diminutive Alain Giresse, had a suspect defence, despite the authoritative play of Marius Tresor. Scotland were thought to have a good chance by their supporters (thousands of whom congregated in the bars of Malaga and Seville) and had an outstanding captain in Graeme Souness but sadly for them one of its few world-class players, Kenny Dalglish, was wretchedly out of form and the defence was sometimes prone to lapses in concentration.

The opening match of the tournament made a refreshing change from the norm. It was the first occasion for 20 years that the result was not a draw and the first occasion since 1950 (when Italy lost in Sao Paulo against Sweden – the Olympic champions two years earlier) that a defending champion had been beaten. The victors were Belgium, who smothered Maradona, used their advantages in height and weight to good purpose, and might easily have scored more than once – the crucial goal coming in the sixty-second minute from Frankie Vercauteren. The pundits who had 'arranged' the Draw six months earlier had been proved mistaken at the first hurdle since it became very unlikely that Argentina would head Group One. (To make matters worse for the players this was soon succeeded by reports that the Falkland Islands had been retaken by the British.) Two days later came a game which witnessed the highest score in the competition when Hungary pulverised El Salvador 10–1, but then followed a match that brought the Hungarians swiftly back to earth when Argentina (with Maradona on outstanding form) beat them 4–1. In turn, Belgium could only put one goal past El Salvador so, given the massive goal-difference that Hungary had built up, victory against the Belgians would have been sufficient to see them through to the Second Round. It was not to be, however, the Hungarians allowing Alex Czerniatynski to grab a reply to an early goal by Joszef Varga. Thus, with Argentina beating El Salvador 2–0 (despite having recaptured their former indifferent form) it was they who accompanied Belgium into the Second Round.

Considerably more dramatic were events in Groups One and Two. The opening match in Group One was a disappointing goalless draw between Italy and Poland which saw a masterly display in the Italian midfield by Giancarlo Antognoni. Poland's star – Boniek – was well marshalled by his future club comrade, Marco Tardelli (who hit the bar during the second half), and there were several half-chances for the Italians. Also goalless was the game between Peru and Cameroon, one of the 'surprise' sides on view. Roger Milla was one of a handful who had gained fame outside his native country due to playing in France but Thomas N'kono turned in a display that showed him to be one of the most gifted goalkeepers in the tournament and in truth Cameroon were unfortunate not to win the game. For Peru the star everyone expected great things from, Julio Cesar Uribe, was a huge disappointment; the much-travelled Teofilo Cubillas was clearly ageing fast and it was only some acrobatic goalkeeping by Ramon Quiroga (known affectionately as 'El Loco') that kept Peru in the game. The side performed with more adventure in its next match against Italy, a 1–1 draw with Toribio Diaz answering an early goal by the effervescent Italian winger, Bruno Conti. Indeed Peru were unlucky not to be awarded a penalty when Juan-Carlos Oblitas was tripped inside the area by Claudio Gentile (of whom more anon!).

The players of Cameroon again displayed their worth by putting on a superb performance against a stilted Poland. Agreed, they had to survive two narrow attempts on their goal from Boniek and the man who had been the top scorer in 1974, Gregorz Lato, but saw several attempts saved by the Poland goalkeeper, Josef Mylnarczk, and it came as little surprise to find Roger Milla (who had played an outstanding game) having his name taken towards the end for throwing the ball in the face of an opponent in sheer frustration.

Only two goals had come in four matches so far and Group One appeared destined to set all sorts of records. The statistics were turned upside down three days later, however, when Poland thrashed Peru 5–1, all the goals coming in the second half of the game. Credit where credit is due – in spite of receiving this pasting, the Peruvian players never allowed themselves to become despondent and, in fact, scored the final goal. It was sad, however, to see an unfit Cubillas – a great star in 1970 when the competition was last held in Mexico – being substituted in the second half. So – to the last game between Italy and Cameroon which would see who would accompany Poland into the Second Round.

Cameroon gained a draw for the third time. Conti blazed over the bar when put through. Collovati and Tardelli saw shots saved by N'kono – and it was only when he slipped that Italy finally managed to score. Within 60 seconds, however, Cameroon had equalised that goal of Graziani's – a rush producing a goal for Gregoire M'bida. Alas for them, however; they were unable to score another – leaving Italy to go through to the Second Round: the two countries had the same number of points but Italy had scored that crucial extra goal. The Cameroon players would have the consolation of being the first team to depart from the competition unbeaten in addition to having given abundant proof of how quickly the game had developed throughout Africa.

Group Two provided still further evidence of this theme with its opening match in which Algeria beat the seeded West Germany by the odd goal in three – a result 'against the form book' that bears comparison with the North Korean victory against Italy in 1966 and the game in the 1950 tournament when England lost to the USA. As with Cameroon, Algeria had several players who belonged to club sides in France in addition to having the current African Footballer of the Year in Lakhdar Belloumi, a 24-year-old midfield player with boundless talent. Their players were also much more used to playing in the humidity experienced in Gijon during the late afternoon. With the skilful Nourredine Kourichi and Mahmoud Gendouz sealing up the middle of the defence the Germans found it almost impossible to carve a way through, so it came as little surprise when a pass from Salah Assad to Belloumi was driven through the German defence, for Rabah Madjer to score after Belloumi's shot had been blocked. It was Belloumi himself who scored the second Algerian goal, sliding a right-foot ball past Harald Schumacher a minute after Karl-Heinz Rummenigge had equalised in the sixty-seventh minute. No more goals, however, and the Germans were left to console themselves with the thought that whenever the country had been victorious it had suffered defeats in the first round: in 1954 by Hungary, in 1974 by East Germany.

Chile showed themselves to be the weakest country in this group, losing 0–1 to Austria and then 1–4 to West Germany, Rummenigge scoring a hat trick. The side also lost to Algeria by the odd goal in five after the Algerians had been beaten 2–0 by Austria. So West Germany positively *had* to win the last game in the Group to be sure of going through to the Second Round. However, if they did so by four goals or more that would permit Algeria to go through on goal difference. Shameful as it was, once the Germans had gone ahead in the tenth minute through Horst Hrubesch, the game came to resemble a match between sleep-walkers, neither side making any effort whatsoever. A disgrace. No wonder the Algerians were incensed – and it raised again the question as to why games should not be played simultaneously (bringing back memories of Argentina's 6–0 victory against Peru in 1978).

In Group Four England made a perfect start when Bryan Robson scored after just 27 seconds against France – the fastest goal in the history of the competition. Although the French replied through Gerard Soler who latched onto a pass from Giresse, Platini had a disappointing match and England were able to finish 3–1, winners thanks to another goal by Robson and one by Paul Mariner. With the plucky Kuwaitis gallantly holding Czechoslovakia to a draw the Group seemed to be smiling on the chances of England qualifying for the Second Round, which hope was confirmed when England beat a demoralised Czechoslovakia 2–0, both goals coming in the second-half. On the debit side, Bryan Robson injured a groin, but as the England manager, Ron Greenwood, pleasantly remarked afterwards the memory of England having qualified 'through the back door' was a thing of the past.

The following day France beat Kuwait 4–1 in the worst-refereed match of the tournament. The Russian official made mistake after mistake, culminating in his disallowing a perfectly good goal by Maxime Bossis, France's left-back, in the sixty-ninth minute when France were already 3–0 in the lead. The Kuwaitis hit back five minutes later but several minutes afterwards came an explosion as the Kuwaitis stopped playing, claiming to have heard a whistle from the crowd signalling that Giresse was off-side when he scored. Bedlam ensued as the referee at first indicated that a goal had been scored – only to change his mind nine minutes later after a protest by the President of the Kuwaiti FA. Three days later France drew 1–1 with the Czechs who had five minutes of frantic hope because Antonin Panenka equalised with a penalty in the eighty-fifth minute. Victory was not forthcoming, however, so it was France who would go through to the Second Stage. The intensity of play during that period was demonstrated by the fact that two minutes afterwards Ladislav Vizek had the ignominy of being the first man to be sent off in the tournament. England finished their spell in the First Round by defeating Kuwait 1–0 so could proudly go forward as one of only two sides to emerge from the First Round with maximum points.

The other side to achieve this feat was Brazil whose first match proved to be one of the best in the tournament. It was against the solid side representing the Soviet Union, which, controlling much of the early play, took the lead in the thirty-third minute through

Andrei Baal. 1–0 the score remained at half-time and long into the second half until Socrates equalised in the seventy-fifth minute with a spectacular shot. 12 minutes later came the final goal from Eder, who collected a pass after Falcao had bewitched his way through the Soviet defence. 2–1 was the final score but this had been a most entertaining match and hopes of neutrals were high that the Soviet Union would progress farther. Certainly, many thought that the refereeing was pitifully inadequate, the Soviet Union being denied two firm claims for a penalty and Brazil one.

24 hours later Scotland beat New Zealand 5–2, a fair result but those two lapses in the defence were to prove costly. When the team met Brazil three days later all returned to milk and honey during the first half-hour as David Narey scored after 18 minutes with a thunderbolt of a shot. That caused Scotland's supporters to feel that their team could go a long way in the tournament; soon after, however, the Brazilians moved up a gear – Zico equalising during the first half – and the second period was almost entirely devoted to the magic of Brazilian football as the South Americans ran in three further goals through Oscar, Eder and Falcao. Since the Soviet Union defeated New Zealand 3–0, Scotland knew that they would have to gain a victory over the USSR to proceed further with their challenge in the tournament. Some wit in the crowd (presumably a Scot!) had made an enormous banner which declaimed the match to be one of ALCOHOLISM versus COMMUNISM and Jock Stein brought back Joe Jordan to remind the Soviets that he meant business. In fact it was Jordan who scored after 15 minutes and, with Graeme Souness organising the side in masterly fashion, a win seemed most possible. But then came one of those failings that so often plague Scotland's goalkeepers when Chivadze, who was not closed down, was given room to strike a shot through a ruck of players; and in the eighty-fourth minute Scotland's central defenders became hopelessly mixed up and allowed Ramon Shengalia enough room to score. Souness made it 2–2 two minutes later but Scotland were eliminated. New Zealand's players found that gallantry was not enough against the Brazilians and went down 0–4 to goals which were among the best in the tournament from Zico and Falcao.

Group Five proved to be most dramatic. According to the form-book both Spain and Yugoslavia would progress easily to the Second Round – convincingly beating Northern Ireland and Honduras. But it was not to be. Honduras announced to everybody that they would not lie down quietly by holding the hosts to a draw, 1–1. Only 24 hours before Hungary had trounced El Salvador, suggesting that both Central American sides might be easy meat! Not so in fact – Honduras scoring after only seven minutes. To equalise, Spain required a penalty and throughout the match displayed apathetic form, while for Honduras Julio Cesar Arzu (in goal) and Allan Costly (in the centre of the defence) showed themselves to be players of the highest class. The following day Northern Ireland drew 0–0 with Yugoslavia, with Norman Whiteside – the youngest player ever to appear in the competition – having a typically robust game in attack and Sammy McIlroy playing his heart out in midfield. Three days later Spain gained that much-desired victory, not against the supposedly-weaker Northern Ireland but instead against Yugoslavia. They required a twice-taken penalty in the fourteenth minute to reply to the Yugoslav goal, which had been scored four minutes earlier by Ivan Gudelj, and it was only a piece of carelessness by Ivica Surjak from a corner in the sixty-sixth minute which permitted the substitute Enrique Saura to race in to score. So Spain won a dull match in which they had played the worse football; in contrast, the following evening came an entertaining 1–1 draw between two of the supposedly weaker sides in the tournament – Honduras and Northern Ireland. Three evenings later the former went on to lose by a single goal to Yugoslavia in a scrappy confrontation, having their midfield player, Gilberto Yearwood, sent off.

The same fate befell Mal Donaghy the day after when Northern Ireland defeated Spain 1–0, Gerry Armstrong scoring just after half-time with the hundredth goal of the tournament. Most referees would have simply booked Donaghy but when you are officiating in the Luis Casanova stadium in Valencia with 50,000 locals wanting blood it can be very easy to be swayed by the crowd – so off Donaghy went. Spain, frankly, were pathetic and only went through to the Second Round as a result of having scored a greater number of goals than Yugoslavia, who also disappointed.

Into the Second Round of the competition went POLAND and ITALY; AUSTRIA and WEST GERMANY; BELGIUM and ARGENTINA; ENGLAND and FRANCE; NORTHERN IRELAND and SPAIN; and BRAZIL and the USSR. Four seeded countries had failed to head their Groups (ITALY, WEST GERMANY, ARGENTINA and SPAIN) but the organisers of the event, must have been most distressed when one of the Second Round groups saw paired together Brazil, Argentina and Italy while Spain, far from being in the supposedly easy group along with Austria and France, saw itself in a group with West Germany and England, both of which were sides Spain feared. Long faces all round.

In Group A a dazzling performance by Boniek helped Poland thrash Belgium 3–0. Moved to play in the attack between Smolarek on the left and the effervescent Lato on the right, Boniek laid on a devastating display of skills and scored a hat-trick of thrilling goals – which almost guaranteed that Poland would go through to the Semi-final stage. That became a certainty after the Soviet Union only managed to beat Belgium 1–0 so that all Poland were required to do in their next game was to hold the winners to a draw. It turned out to be a 'Goalless Grimmie'; one of the few highlights off the pitch being the appearance of several banners supporting Solidarity, which were removed, presumably on the orders of the Soviet authorities.

Group B started with a goalless draw between West Germany and England – a result that suited Spain, whose players turned up half-an-hour before the kick-off and received the loudest cheer of the night. The match proved to be a disappointing contest, England's best football coming during the first half when Harald Schumacher was forced to make crucial saves from Ray Wilkins and Bryan Robson, but as the game went on the English players began to tire quickly in the strength-sapping heat. Three days later West Germany beat Spain 2–1 in a game that saw much more action than the first contest. Zamora returned after injury but the other Spanish player of flair, Juanito, was injured just before half-time and substituted, leaving the host country without ideas of how to get goals. West Germany, on the other hand, really

sparked for the first time in this competition – Pierre Littbarski, on
viperish form in the forward line, opening the scoring just after
half-time. A welcome goal, particularly given that Rummenigge
had been unable to come out after the interval. With Klaus Fischer
adding a second in the seventy-fifth minute, Zamora's goal for
Spain appeared to be almost an irrelevancy.

So England had to play Spain, seeking to win by two clear goals
or by 3–2 or 4–3: a difference that would permit them to overtake
the Germans. Sadly for them they could manage nothing better
than a goalless draw – with misses taking place at each end. In the
sixty-third minute Ron Greenwood brought on Trevor Brooking
and Kevin Keegan but while Brooking looked sharp and creative,
Kevin Keegan just failed to glance into the Spanish goal a cross
from Bryan Robson and clearly lacked match-fitness. 0–0 therefore, and England were out (as were Spain) but with the satisfaction of being unbeaten. If only Brooking and Keegan had been fit
throughout. In the end, however, England could only blame their
inability to take the chances offered.

Group C saw the meeting of three of the Titans in the history of
the tournament – and every match proved to be full of interest.
Italy met Argentina in a bruiser of a contest which saw five players
being booked – two Italian, three Argentinian – one where so often
footballing skills became submerged by the importance of the
occasion. The entire first-half, in fact, was taken up with the two
sides testing each other out but Italy took the lead in the fifty-sixth
minute in dramatic fashion – Antognoni slipping through a perfect
pass for his midfield colleague, Tardelli, to race through and
score. As the Argentinian players strove to equalise, sadly for
them, they left gaps in their defence and after Ubaldo Fillol had
fouled Paolo Rossi, Bruno Conti retrieved the ball and gave it to
the oncoming Antonio Cabrini to score. Although the Argentine
captain, Daniel Passarella, pulled back a goal, 2–1 was the final
score. Thus it would be Argentina who would perform next against
their arch-rivals Brazil, but would be prevented from calling on
their midfield player, Amerigo Gallego, who had been dismissed
from the field five minutes from the end.

Matches between the two South-American countries are always

tense – and this particular match was no exception to that dictum. It was almost killed stone-dead, however, in the eleventh minute when Eder bent a free-kick from 30 metres out against the bar, only for Zico to scramble the ball home. Two further scores came from the Brazilians in the second-half but there came only a solitary reply by Ramon Diaz in the last minute to make the score 3–1. Maradona in the previous match had been forced to endure some savage tackling on the part of Claudio Gentile but in this match he committed a foul on Batista of which Gentile would have been proud, and was sent off for his pains. He turned out to have experienced a most disappointing World Cup, his only match of note having been the game against Hungary.

Three days later followed a match which will enter the Pantheon of outstanding games in the history of the tournament when Italy beat Brazil 3–2 in a totally absorbing contest. Paolo Rossi suddenly came into electrifying form in the attack, scoring all three Italian goals – his first in the competition – and Giancarlo Antognoni can have had few better games in the Italian midfield. Rossi scored after five and 25 minutes (following a crass mistake by the Brazilian defence) but Brazil replied dramatically after 12 minutes through Socrates and 68 minutes when Falcao scored one of the goals of the championship, shimmering his way through the Italian defence. With Gentile giving Zico a dose of the treatment he had meted out a week earlier to Maradona, one of the principal threats to Italy was shackled as firmly as had been the Argentinian. When Falcao's goal was scored the hearts of many Italian supporters must have sunk but such had been the spirit of determination induced in his players by Enzo Bearzot, the Italian manager, that anything seemed possible and it was 'The Prodigal Son' who scored the third goal six minutes later which took Italy into the Semi-final stage, where they would play Poland, with whom they had played a goalless draw in the First Round. On this occasion, however, it would be essential to win.

Group D saw Northern Ireland initially waiting on the sidelines while France played Austria. Now the knock-out principle was partly in use (the losers of a Group match automatically going on to play in the following match), the French team started to display what it was capable of. With Alain Giresse in corruscating form in midfield and Dominique Rocheteau becoming sharper in attack, with Marius Tresor displaying all his experience at centre-back and with many of the Austrians playing as if in a comatose state, France was able to dominate an entertaining game, although only scoring once when Bernard Genghini curled in a direct free kick that stunned the Austrian defence. Three days later, another lively match between Northern Ireland and Austria finished as a 2–2 draw, the Ulster men deservedly taking the lead through Billy Hamilton who put in a second after Austria had scored twice in the second half. Neither team, however, was able to add a decisive third goal so that when they met France three days later Northern Ireland knew they required a victory to be sure of reaching the Semi-final stage.

Unfortunately for them, Northern Ireland had to play in broiling conditions which they found most taxing. France, at last enjoying a streak of glorious form, took the lead in the thirty-third minute thanks to Giresse who tapped home a cross from Michel Platini, having his best match to date in the competition. Rocheteau added two further goals before Armstrong was able to score for the Irish but with a win being necessary, the hope of scoring three further goals in the last 16 minutes was beyond the realms of possibility and at the finish France went through 4–1, Giresse heading home in the eightieth minute. The Irish were eliminated from the tournament but could hold their heads high, while for the first time since 1958 France had reached the last four in the World Cup and would advance to the Semi-final stage, in which they would meet West Germany. (Even the valiant goal-keeper, Pat Jennings, could do nothing.)

This was the first occasion since 1966 that all four Semi-finalists came from Europe. The less intricate of the games saw a revitalised Italy beating Poland 2–0 in the Nou Camp stadium at Barcelona, both goals being scored by Paolo Rossi, who seemed to have completely rediscovered his instincts as a predator. The Polish players appeared to enter the game with an attitude that was totally pessimistic. Agreed, the heat was more taxing to them than it was to the Italians; agreed the suspension of their most gifted player – Boniek – had been a crucial blow. However, on the other hand, Antognoni was forced to leave the field injured in the twenty-ninth minute, seven minutes after Rossi had scored his first goal, causing a certain amount of reorganisation in the Italian side. But Poland were unable to take advantage of that piece of fortune, the only threat to the Italian goal coming from long-range shooting by the Polish midfield player Janusz Kupcewicz. In the seventy-third minute a classic header by Rossi from a centre by Conti sewed up the match for Italy who thus became the first team to appear in four Finals in the year history of the World Cup.

Soon after, Italy would have to share that record with West Germany but the other Semi-final deserves a chapter on its own for containing superb drama in addition to heart-bursting emotion. Just examine the scoreline: 1–1 at half-time, 1–1 at full time, 3–3 after extra-time – so the contest had to be resolved by a penalty shoot-out. An engrossing contest, this between German organisation and French skill, with Michel Platini at last playing at the peak of his form. It was Platini, in fact, who scored France's equaliser ten minutes after Littbarski had given West Germany the lead in the seventeenth minute, hitting home a penalty. Although the match continued to thrill, the crucial moment came in the fifty-sixth minute when Platini hit a superb pass through the German defence for Patrick Battiston – who had come on only six minutes earlier as a substitute – to run on unmarked towards the German goal. That was when Schumacher chose to come out at speed and – with no attempt to play the ball – to clummock Battiston to the ground, unconscious and minus two teeth. It took over three minutes for a stretcher to be brought onto the field (so security-conscious were the authorities that the Red Cross officials had been banned from the pitch), which delay served to make the incident seem even more dramatic.

Instead of being dismissed from the field by the Dutch referee, Corver, the German goalkeeper was simply shown a yellow card – which fact appeared even more shameful as the game went into extra-time. During that period France took a 3–1 lead, thanks to goals by Tresor and Giresse, only for West Germany to equalise through Rummenigge (who had just come on as a substitute) and

Fischer. 3–3 then, and the first penalty shoot-out in the history of the tournament saw each side strike home four of its first five attempts to score – Stielike and then Six going through the agony of seeing their shots saved by the opposing goalkeeper. It became an affair of sudden-death at that stage with poor Maxime Bossis next in line: his shot smacked against the bar and rebounded into play. Hrubesch made no mistake with his shot – and West Germany proceeded to its second Final in three World Cups fully aware that Dame Fortune had been smiling on them, instead of on the unfortunate French.

Little wonder that when the Third Place match took place two days later France took the field against Poland with only four of the men who had started the match against West Germany – the tireless Marius Tresor, Amoros, Janvion (in defence) and Jean Tigana (in midfield). It turned out to be an entertaining contest which they would lose but only by the odd goal in five. France, in fact, took the lead in the twelfth minute through Girard but another old favourite from the side that had come third in 1974, Andrzej Szarmach, replied in the fortieth minute when he scored after accepting a telling pass by Boniek. Seconds before half-time Majewski headed in a second which was followed two minutes after the interval by a curling free-kick by Kupcewicz. 3–1 to Poland, then, with three goals having come in the space of seven minutes. France, however, then sprang to the challenge, mounting attack after attack and Alain Couriol made it 3–2 in the seventy-third minute. Which made for a dramatic final seventeen minutes as France attempted to score an equaliser. It was not to be but neutrals would point out that France had been forced to play only forty-eight hours after that traumatic meeting with West Germany in addition to having been exhausted by playing that particular encounter in the heat of Madrid instead of the comparative cool of Barcelona.

The same argument might also be applied to West Germany in the Final the following day. But few felt much sympathy for the Germans, having seen them beaten in their opening match by Algeria, and two games later coming that insult of a match between West Germany and Austria. The Germans even had fortune on their side in the Final when Giancarlo Antognoni was declared unfit at the last minute and received a further slice of luck since Graziani had to be helped off the field in the seventh minute when he injured a shoulder. Their largest slice of good fortune came in the twenty-fourth minute when Cabrini sliced wide a penalty-kick after Briegel had pulled down Conti inside the area, the first-ever penalty miss in the history of the competition. Conti, in fact, was Italy's most dangerous attacker and came close to scoring on several occasions but the first half finished goalless.

What a pleasing change in the second-half! Italy took the lead in the fifty-sixth minute when Rossi hit home at the near-post after a cross from Gentile, and that goal was added to 12 minutes later as Tardelli shot home after Gentile had finished a glorious move by the Italian midfield. 12 minutes after *that*, as the Germans allowed their discipline to wander after Briegel had been refused a penalty, Bruno Conti sprinted more than half the length of the field to put across a perfect pass for Altobelli to shoot past Schumacher. Although West Germany scored in the eighty-second minute through Brietner, Bearzot had the last word by putting on as substitute one of his favourites in the squad, Franco Causio, with only two minutes to play.

When Dino Zoff lifted the World Cup trophy soon after, he became only the second goalkeeper to captain a victorious side (the first being his fellow-countryman Giampiero Combi in 1934). Few could argue that Italy had not deserved to take the trophy for the third time, the first European country to achieve this feat. The form displayed by the side during the First Round had distressed its many followers throughout the world, and Enzo Bearzot must have given a vast sigh of relief when the match against Cameroon was finished and Italy were sure of progressing in the tournament. To be drawn at the Second Stage, however alongside those giants from South America, Brazil and Argentina, must have provided a fresh torment. Both teams possessed individuals of great talent who were capable of creating a goal out of nothing. Enter Claudio Gentile who by means fair or foul (very often the latter) entirely shackled up first Diego Maradona of Argentina and then Zico of Brazil. He was extremely fortunate not

Pelé and Bobby Moore exchange shirts after Brazil had beaten England 1-0 in the 1970 World Cup.

Francis Lee busy in action during the Quarter-final game in the 1970 World Cup which England lost 2-3 in extra time after having led 2-0. Those watching are Brian Labone, Klaus Fichtel, Franz Beckenbauer, Sepp Maier, Uwe Seeler and Berti Vogts.

World Cup Final 1970. Jairzinho moments after he had
scored Brazil's third goal. Pelé is the other Brazilian player
while the Italians are Mazzola, Facchetti, Burgnich and De
Sisti.

The face of Billy Bremner tells the story as he watches his shot
skimming just past on the wrong side of the Brazilian goal.
Leao is the beaten goalkeeper, Hay and Piazza the other players.

Johann Cruyff on the right, moments after scoring the
second of Holland's goals in the 2-0 victory against Brazil.
The other Dutch player is Johnny Rep.

Roberto Bettega scores the single goal of the game in which
Italy inflicted a defeat on Argentina.

Daniel Bertoni races away after scoring Argentina's last goal in the 3-1 victory over Holland in the 1978 Final. The other players are Mario Kempès, Leopoldo Luque and the beaten goalkeeper is Jan Jongbloed, who is appealing for offside.

Bryan Robson scoring the fastest goal in the history of the tournament after only 27 seconds against France. Jean-Luc Ettori is the hapless goalkeeper.

Lakhdar Belloumi scoring Algeria's second goal against
West Germany. Algeria eventually won 2-1, causing one of
the biggest upsets in the history of the competition.

Alexandr Chivadze of the USSR scoring the first of their
goals in the 2-2 draw against Scotland. The Scotland
players are Willie Miller, John Wark, John Robertson and
Alan Hansen.

Gerry Armstrong scoring the only goal of the match when
Northern Ireland defeated Spain. It was the hundredth goal
of the 1982 World Cup.

Zbigniew Boniek scoring his third goal as Poland beat
Belgium 3-0 in a match from the Second Round. The other
Polish player is Lato who played his hundredth game
during the tournament on the right wing.

Antonio Cabrini and Gaetano Scirea (No. 7) watching as
Claudio Gentile of Italy decidedly does *not* live up to his
name. The victim is Diego Maradona of Argentina. In the
following match the Italian turned his attentions to the
Brazilian, Zico.

Paolo Rossi slides the ball past the Brazilian goalkeeper,
Waldir Peres, to score his third goal in the 3-2 victory over
the Brazilians. In the background are Socrates of Brazil
(who replied to Rossi's first goal) and Giancarlo Antognoni
of Italy who also had an outstanding match.

A scene from the West Germany-France Semi-final in which Michel Platini of France is challenged by Manfred Kaltz of West Germany.

World Cup Final 1982. Two of the most accomplished players in the competition – Bruno Conti of Italy and Hans-Peter Briegel of West Germany. Conti's play on the right side of the Italian attack did much to aid Paolo Rossi, the chief scorer in the tournament.

to be dismissed from the field but the psychological impact of his rigid marking was enormous.

In addition, Bearzot knew that he had another ace up his sleeve, an ace called Paolo Rossi who, with every game he played, was getting rid of the cobwebs of having been out of action for the past two years. Giancarlo Antognoni had slotted back into the side in a masterly fashion after having been out of the game for several months with a head injury and the faith that Bearzot also held for Rossi was justly rewarded by the thrilling goals which he scored in those last three games. Above all, Bearzot, not a spiteful man, must have received a fair amount of glee from reading the copy in the sports papers and pages from correspondents having to swallow their words. Not a few of those – even as late as May – had called for him to be replaced as manager.

Italy had the highest number of players booked in the competition (11) but theirs was a triumph for spirit over adversity; they splendidly beat Brazil, the team favoured by many as well as that which had scored most goals in the tournament (15) and although the Final tended to disappoint, few could doubt Italy were worthy champions.

1982 Final Stages

Second Stage

Group A

	P	W	D	L	F	A	Pts
POLAND	2	1	1	0	3	0	3
USSR	2	0	1	0	1	0	3
BELGIUM	2	0	0	2	0	4	0

Group B

WEST GERMANY	2	1	1	0	2	1	3
ENGLAND	2	0	2	0	0	0	2
SPAIN	2	0	1	1	1	2	1

Group C

ITALY	2	2	0	0	5	3	4
BRAZIL	2	1	0	1	5	4	2
ARGENTINA	2	0	0	2	2	5	0

Group D

FRANCE	2	2	0	0	5	1	4
AUSTRIA	2	0	1	1	2	3	1
NORTHERN IRELAND	2	0	1	1	2	6	1

Semi-Final Stage

POLAND 0, ITALY 2 (0–1) Rossi (2) for Italy

POLAND: Mylnarczyk, Dziuba, Zmuda, Janas, Majewski, Kupcewicz, Buncol, Matysik, Lato, Ciolek (Palasz), Smolarek (Kusto).
ITALY: Zoff, Bergomi, Collovati, Scirea, Cabrini, Oriali, Antognoni (Marini), Tardelli, Conti, Rossi, Graziani (Altobelli).

WEST GERMANY 3, FRANCE 3 (1–1) aet, Littbarski, Rummenigge, Fischer for West Germany; Platini (pen.), Tresor,
Giresse for France

WEST GERMANY: Schumacher, Kaltz, Förster K. H., Stielike,
Förster B., Briegel (Rummenigge), Dremmler, Brietner, Littbarski, Fischer, Magath (Hrubesch).
FRANCE: Ettori, Amoros, Janvion, Tresor, Bossis, Genghini (Battiston then Lopez), Platini, Giresse, Rocheteau, Six, Tigana.

West Germany won 5–4 on penalties: Kaltz, Brietner, Littbarski,
Rummenigge and Hrubesch scored as did Giresse, Amoros,
Rocheteau and Platini. Stielike's shot was saved as were those of
Six and Bossis for France.

Third Place Match played in Alicante

POLAND 3, FRANCE 2 (2–1) Szarmach, Majewski, Buncol for
Poland; Girard, Couriol for France

POLAND: Mylnarczyk, Dziuba, Janas, Zmuda, Majewski, Kupce-
wicz, Matysik (Wojicki), Lato, Buncol, Boniek, Szarmach.
FRANCE: Castaneda, Amoros, Mahut, Tresor, Janvion (Lopez),
Tigana (Six), Larios, Girard, Couriol, Soler, Bellone.

Final played in Madrid

ITALY 3, WEST GERMANY 1 (0–0) Rossi, Tardelli, Altobelli
for Italy, Breitner for West Germany

ITALY: Zoff, Gentile, Collovati, Scirea, Cabrini, Oriali, Bergomi,
Tardelli, Conti, Rossi, Graziani (Altobelli then Causio).
WEST GERMANY: Schumacher, Kaltz, Förster K. H., Stielike,
Briegel, Dremmler (Hrubesch), Breitner, Förster B., Rumme-
nigge (Müller), Fischer, Littbarski.

5 SOME STATISTICS

Number of Entries

1930 in Uruguay – 13
1934 in Italy – 32
1938 in France – 36
1950 in Brazil – 32
1954 in Switzerland – 38
1958 in Sweden – 53
1962 in Chile – 56
1966 in England – 71
1970 in Mexico – 70
1974 in West Germany – 99
1978 in Argentina – 106
1982 in Spain – 109

Attendances at Final Matches

1930 at Montevideo – 90,000   URUGUAY 4 ARGENTINA 2
1934 at Rome – 50,000   ITALY 2 CZECHOSLOVAKIA 1
(after extra time)
1938 at Paris – 45,000   ITALY 4 HUNGARY 2
1950 at Rio de Janeiro – 199,850   URUGUAY 2 BRAZIL 1
1954 at Berne – 60,000   WEST GERMANY 3 HUNGARY 2
1958 at Stockholm – 49,737   BRAZIL 5 SWEDEN 2
1962 at Santiago – 68,679   BRAZIL 3 CZECHOSLOVAKIA 1
1966 at London – 93,802   ENGLAND 4 WEST GERMANY 2
(after extra time)
1970 at Mexico City – 107,412   BRAZIL 4 ITALY 1
1974 at Munich – 77,833   WEST GERMANY 2 HOLLAND 1
1978 at Buenos Aires – 77,000   ARGENTINA 3 HOLLAND 1
(after extra time)
1982 at Madrid – 90,089   ITALY 3 WEST GERMANY 1

Analysis of the winning teams in the World Cup

		P	W	D	L	F	A

1930 URUGUAY   4 4 0 0 15 3
15 players used. Ballesteros, Nasazzi, Cea, Andrade (J), Fernandez, Gestido, Iriarte 4 apps. each; Dorado, Mascheroni, Scarone 3 each; Castro, Anselmo 2 each; Tejera, Petrone, Urdinaran 1 each.

1934 ITALY   5 4 1 0 12 3
17 players used. Combi, Allemandi, Monti, Meazza, Orsi 5 each; Monzeglio, Bertolini, Schiavio, Ferrari, Guiata 4 each; Ferraris IV 3; Pizziolo 2; Rosetta, Guarisi, Castellazzi, Borel, Demaris 1 each.

1938 ITALY   4 4 0 0 11 5
14 players used. Olivieri, Rava, Serantoni, Andreolo, Locatelli, Meazza, Piolo, Ferrari 4 each; Foni, Biavati, Colaussi 3 each; Monzeglio, Pasinati, Ferraris 1 each.

1950 URUGUAY   4 3 1 0 15 5
14 players used. Gonzales M., Tejera, Valera, Andrade R., Ghiggia, Perez, Miguez, Schiaffino 4 each; Maspoli, Vidal 3 each; Gonzales W., Gambetta 2 each; Paz, Moran 1 each.

1954 WEST GERMANY   6 5 0 1 25 14
18 players used. Eckel, Walter F. 6 each; Turek, Kohlmeyer, Posipal, Mai, Morlock, Walter O., Schafer 5 each; Liebrich, Rahn 4 each; Laband 3; Klodt, Bauer 2 each; Mebus, Herrmann, Kwaitowski, Pfaff 1 each.

1958 BRAZIL   6 5 1 0 16 4
16 players used. Gilmar, Nilton Santos, Bellini, Orlando, Didi, Zagalo 6 each; De Sordi 5; Vavà, Zito, Garrincha, Pelé 4 each; Mazzola 3; Dino, Joel 2 each; Djalma Santos, Didì 1 each.

		P	W	D	L	F	A
1962	BRAZIL	6	5	1	0	14	5

12 players used (the lowest number by any Winner). Gilmar, Santos
D., Santos N., Zozimo, Mauro, Zito, Didì, Vava, Garrincha,
Zagalo 6 each; Amarildo 4; Pelé 2.

		P	W	D	L	F	A
1966	ENGLAND	6	5	1	0	14	3

15 players used. Banks, Cohen, Wilson, Stiles, Charlton J., Moore,
Hunt, Charlton R. 6 each; Peters 5; Ball 4; Greaves, Hurst 3 each;
Paine, Callaghan, Connelly 1 each.

		P	W	D	L	F	A
1970	BRAZIL	6	6	0	0	19	7

16 players used. Felix, Carlos Alberto, Piazza, Brito, Clodoaldo,
Jairzinho, Pelé, Tostao 6 each; Everaldo, Rivelino 5 each; Gerson
4; Paulo Cesar 2 + 2 subs; Marco Antonio 1 + 1 sub; Roberto 2
subs; Fontana 1; Edu 1 sub.

		P	W	D	L	F	A
1974	WEST GERMANY	7	6	0	1	13	4

18 players used. Maier, Vogts, Breitner, Schwarzenbeck, Beckenbauer, Muller, Overath 7 each; Hoeness 6 + 1 sub; Grabowski 5
+ 1 sub; Bonhof 4; Holzenbein 4 + 2 subs; Cullman 3; Heynckes,
Herzog 2 each; Flohe 1 + 2 subs; Wimmer 1 + 1 sub; Netzer,
Hottges 1 sub each.

		P	W	D	L	F	A
1978	ARGENTINA	7	5	1	1	15	4

17 players used. Fillol, Galvan L., Olguin, Passarella, Tarantini,
Gallego, Kempès 7 each; Ardiles 6; Bertoni 5 + 1 sub; Ortiz 4 + 2
subs; Luque 5; Houseman 3 + 3 subs; Valencia 4; Larrosa 1 + 1
sub; Alonso 3 subs; Villa 2 subs.

		P	W	D	L	F	A
1982	ITALY	7	4	3	0	12	6

15 players used. Zoff, Cabrini, Collovati, Scirea, Conti B., Tardelli,
Rossi, Graziani 7 each; Antognoni, Gentile 6 each; Oriali 5;
Marini 2 + 3 subs; Bergomi 2 + 1 sub; Altobelli 3 subs; Causio 2
subs.

Leading Scorers

1930   8 STABILE (Argentina)
        5 CEA (Uruguay)

1934   4 SCHIAVIO (Italy), CONEN (Germany) and NEJEDLY (Czechoslovakia)

1938   8 LEONIDAS (Brazil)
        7 SZENGELLER (Hungary)
        5 PIOLA (Italy)

1950   7 ADEMIR (Brazil)
        5 SCHIAFFINO (Uruguay), BASORA (Spain)

1954   11 KOCSIS (Hungary)
        6 MQRLOCK (West Germany), PROBST (Austria)
        5 HUGI (Switzerland)

1958   13 FONTAINE (France)
        6 PELÉ (Brazil), RAHN (West Germany)
        5 VAVA (Brazil), McPARLAND (Northern Ireland)

1962   5 JERKOVIC (Yugoslavia)
        4 ALBERT (Hungary), GARRINCHA (Brazil), IVANOV (USSR),
           SANCHEZ (Chile), VAVA (Brazil)

1966   9 EUSEBIO (Portugal)
        5 HALLER (West Germany)
        4 HURST (England), BENE (Hungary), PORKUIAN (USSR),
           BECKENBAUER (West Germany)

1970   10 MÜLLER (West Germany)
        7 JAIRZINHO (Brazil) who scored in each game played by the Winners
        5 CUBILLAS (Peru)

1974   7 LATO (Poland)
        5 SZARMACH (Poland), NEESKENS (Holland)
        4 MULLER (West Germany), REP (Holland), EDSTROEM (Sweden)

1978   6 KEMPÈS (Argentina)
        5 RENSENBRINK (Holland), CUBILLAS (Peru)
        4 LUQUE (Argentina), KRANKL (Austria)

1982   6 ROSSI (Italy)
        5 RUMMENIGGE (West Germany)
        4 BONIEK (Poland), ZICO (Brazil)

Placed together the best individual goal-scoring performances in the World Cup Final tournaments go like this:

13 Fontaine 1958
11 Kocsis 1954
10 Muller 1970
 9 Eusebio 1966
 8 Stabile 1930
   Leonidas 1938

7 Szengeller 1938
  Ademir 1950
  Jairzinho 1970
  Lato 1974
6 Probst 1954
  Morlock 1954
  Pelé 1958
  Rahn 1958
  Kempes 1978
  Rossi 1982

The catalogue of best all-time goal-scorers is as follows:

14 Muller (West Germany) in 1970 and 1974
13 Fontaine (France) in 1958
12 Pelé (Brazil) in 1958, 1962, 1966 and 1970
11 Kocsis (Hungary) in 1954
10 Cubillas (Peru) in 1970 and 1978
   Lato (Poland) in 1974, 1978 and 1982
   Rahn (West Germany) in 1954 and 1958
 9 Eusebio (Portugal) in 1966
   Jairzinho (Brazil) in 1970 and 1974
   Rossi (Italy) in 1978 and 1982
   Seeler (West Germany) in 1958, 1962, 1966 and 1970
   Vava (Brazil) in 1958 and 1962
 8 Leonidas (Brazil) in 1938
   Stabile (Argentina) in 1930

Some Interesting Records

ANTONIO CARBAJAL (Mexico) is the player to have appeared in most World Cup tournaments. He kept goal in 1950, 1954, 1958, 1962 and 1966

UWE SEELER (West Germany) is the player to have appeared in most matches playing on 21 occasions in the Finals of 1958, 1962, 1966 and 1970.

MARIO ZAGALO (Brazil) is the only man so far to have played in (1958 and 1962) and managed (1970) winning teams.

FRANZ BECKENBAUER (West Germany) is the only manager of a team that has qualified for the 1986 finals who saw action in the previous tournament to be held in Mexico. Beckenbauer took part in five of the six matches played by his country before being declared unfit. He appeared against Morocco, Bulgaria, Peru, England and Italy.

BRYAN ROBSON (England) became the scorer of the *fastest goal* in the history of the World Cup when he scored after only 27 seconds in the match against France on 16 June 1982.

NORMAN WHITESIDE (Northern Ireland) became the *youngest* player ever to compete in a World Cup Final tournament when he played against Yugoslavia on 17 June 1982.

When PORTUGAL defeated WEST GERMANY by 1–0 on 16 October 1985, it was the first occasion that the country had been beaten in the Qualifying Rounds of a World Cup tournament (it failed to enter in 1930, was banned from entry 20 years later and was victorious in the 1954 and the 1974 editions of the tournament, the last of which it hosted). Before this historic defeat it had won 32 and drawn four of its 36 matches. A truly astonishing record.

GEOFF HURST (England) is the only player to date to have scored a hat-trick in a World Cup Final but the record for scoring goals in any World Cup match is four, a feat which has been achieved on eight occasions:

GUSTAV WETTERSTROEM   Sweden v Cuba 1938
LEONIDAS DA SILVA   Brazil v Poland 1938
ERNEST WILLIMOWSKI   Poland v Brazil 1938
ADEMIR   Brazil v Sweden 1950
JUAN SCHIAFFINO   Uruguay v Bolivia 1950
SANDOR KOCSIS   Hungary v West Germany 1954
JUST FONTAINE   France v West Germany 1958
EUSEBIO   Portugal v North Korea 1966

Goal milestones in the World Cup

1st goal: LAURENT (France) 13 July 1930 against Mexico (4–1)
100th goal: JONASSON (Sweden) 1934 against Argentina (3–2)
200th goal: WETTERSTROEM (Sweden) 1938 against Cuba (8–0)
300th goal: CHICO (Brazil) 1950 against Spain (6–1)
400th goal: LEFTER (Turkey) 1954 against West Germany (2–7)
500th goal: RAHN (West Germany) 1958 against Czechoslovakia
(2–2)
600th goal: JERKOVIC (Yugoslavia) 1962 against Hungary (3–1)
700th goal: BOBBY CHARLTON (England) 1966 against Mexico
(2–0)
800th goal: JAIRZINHO (Brazil) 1970 against England (1–0)
900th goal: YAZALDE (Argentina) 1974 against Haiti (4–1)
1000th goal: RENSENBRINK (Holland) 1978 against Scotland
(2–3)
1100th goal: BLOKHIN (USSR) 1982 against New Zealand (3–0)
1200th goal: ....
1300th goal: ....

Attendances and Goals World Cup 1930–1978

YEAR	VENUE	ATTENDANCES	AVERAGE	MATCHES	GOALS	AVERAGE
1930	URUGUAY	434,500	24,139	18	70	3.88
1934	ITALY	395,000	23,235	17	70	4.11
1938	FRANCE	483,000	26,833	18	84	4.66
1950	BRAZIL	1,337,000	60,772	22	88	4.00
1954	SWITZERLAND	943,000	36,270	26	140	5.38
1958	SWEDEN	868,000	24,800	35	126	3.60
1962	CHILE	776,000	24,250	32	89	2.78
1966	ENGLAND	1,614,677	50,458	32	89	2.78
1970	MEXICO	1,673,975	52,312	32	95	2.96
1974	WEST GERMANY	1,774,022	46,685	38	97	2.55
1978	ARGENTINA	1,610,215	42,374	38	102	2.68
1982	SPAIN	1,766,277	33,967	52	146	2.8

The Trophy

The Jules Rimet Trophy – won outright by the Brazilians in 1970
on account of their third victory – was designed by the French
sculptor, Abel Lafleur, stood a foot high and weighed in the region
of nine pounds of gold. The present trophy – competed for in 1974
for the first time and known as the FIFA World Cup – was designed
by an Italian, Silvio Gazzaniga, cost £8,000, was made in eighteen-
carat gold and weighs about ten pounds.

Only six countries have won the World Cup:

Brazil (1958, 1962 and 1970),
Italy (1934, 1938 and 1982),
Uruguay (1930 and 1950),
West Germany (1954 and 1974),
England (1966),
and Argentina (1978)

Of these, Brazil is the only country to have gained all her victories
away from home (she unexpectedly lost the 1950 Final match
to Uruguay in Rio de Janeiro) in addition to being the only
country to succeed in different continents (Sweden in 1958 and
Mexico in 1970).

'Host' countries for the final stages have been:

Uruguay (1930)
Italy (1934)
England (1966)
West Germany (1974)
and Argentina (1978)

*The only players to have the distinction of gaining winners' medals in
TWO World Cups are:*

GIOVANNI FERRARI (Italy 1934 and 1938)
GIUSEPPE MEAZZA (Italy 1934 and 1938)
and
PELÉ (Brazil 1958 and 1970) – the only man to have scored in two
Finals.

Expulsions During Previous Tournaments

URUGUAY 1930	Cierro (Argentina)
FRANCE 1938	Machados and Zeze (Brazil) Riha (Czechoslovakia)
SWITZERLAND 1954	Nilton Santos and Tozzi (Brazil) Bozsik (Hungary)
SWEDEN 1958	Bubernik (Czechoslovakia) Sipos (Hungary) Juskowiak (West Germany)
CHILE 1962	David and Ferrini (Italy)
ENGLAND 1966	Rattin (Argentina) Silva and Troche (Uruguay)
WEST GERMANY 1974	Caszely (Chile) Richards (Australia) Ndaye (Zaire) Montero Castillo (Uruguay) Luis Pereira (Brazil)
ARGENTINA 1978	Nyilasi and Toroscik (Hungary) Naninga (Holland)
SPAIN 1982	Vizek (Czechoslovakia), Gilberto Yearwood (Honduras), Donaghy (Northern Ireland), Gallego and Maradona (Argentina)

6 SUMMARY OF MATCHES IN WORLD CUP FINALS 1930–1982

		Part.	Gms.	W	D	L	F	A	Pts.
* 1.	BRAZIL	12	57	37	10	10	134	62	84
* 2.	WEST GERMANY	10	54	32	10	12	122	78	74
* 3.	ITALY	10	43	24	9	10	74	46	57
* 4.	ARGENTINA	8	34	16	5	13	63	51	37
* 5.	ENGLAND	7	29	13	8	8	40	29	34
* 6.	URUGUAY	7	29	14	5	10	57	39	33
* 7.	HUNGARY	8	29	14	3	12	85	48	31
* 8.	USSR	5	24	12	5	7	37	25	29
* 9.	POLAND	4	21	12	4	5	38	22	28
10.	YUGOSLAVIA	7	28	11	6	11	47	36	28
11.	SWEDEN	7	28	11	6	11	48	46	28
*12.	FRANCE	8	27	11	2	14	59	50	24
13.	AUSTRIA	5	23	11	2	10	38	39	24
*14.	SPAIN	6	23	8	5	10	26	30	21
15.	CZECHOSLOVAKIA	7	25	8	5	12	34	40	21
16.	HOLLAND	4	16	8	3	5	32	19	19
17.	CHILE	5	18	7	3	8	23	24	17
18.	SWITZERLAND	6	18	5	2	11	28	44	12
19.	PERU	4	15	4	3	8	19	31	11
*20.	SCOTLAND	5	14	3	5	6	20	29	11
*21.	PORTUGAL	1	6	5	0	1	17	8	10
*22.	NORTHERN IRELAND	2	10	3	4	3	11	17	10
*23.	MEXICO	8	24	3	4	17	21	62	10
*24.	BELGIUM	6	14	3	2	9	15	30	8
25.	EAST GERMANY	1	6	2	2	2	5	5	6
*26.	PARAGUAY	3	7	2	2	3	12	19	6
27.	USA	3	7	3	0	4	12	21	6
28.	WALES	1	5	1	3	1	4	4	5

29.	RUMANIA	4	8	2	1	5	12	17	5
*30.	ALGERIA	1	3	2	0	1	5	5	4
*31.	BULGARIA	4	12	0	4	8	9	29	4
32.	TUNISIA	1	3	1	1	1	3	2	3
33.	CAMEROON	1	3	0	3	0	1	1	3
34.	NORTH KOREA	1	4	1	1	2	5	9	3
35.	CUBA	1	3	1	1	1	5	12	3
36.	HONDURAS	1	3	0	2	1	2	3	2
37.	TURKEY	1	3	1	0	2	10	11	2
38.	ISRAEL	1	3	0	2	1	1	3	2
39.	KUWAIT	1	3	0	1	2	2	6	1
*40.	MOROCCO	1	3	0	1	2	1	6	1
41.	AUSTRALIA	1	3	0	1	2	0	5	1
42.	COLOMBIA	1	3	0	1	2	5	11	1
43.	IRAN	1	3	0	1	2	2	8	1
44.	NORWAY	1	1	0	0	1	1	2	0
45.	EGYPT	1	1	0	0	1	2	4	0
46.	DUTCH EAST INDIES	1	1	0	0	1	0	6	0
47.	NEW ZEALAND	1	3	0	0	3	2	12	0
48.	HAITI	1	3	0	0	3	2	14	0
49.	ZAIRE	1	3	0	0	3	0	14	0
*50.	SOUTH KOREA	1	2	0	0	2	0	16	0
51.	BOLIVIA	2	3	0	0	3	0	16	0
52.	EL SALVADOR	2	6	0	0	6	1	22	0

* *Countries that have qualified*

BRAZIL remain the only country to have taken part in every final competition of the World Cup. And it is interesting to note the fact that PORTUGAL in their one appearance to date acquired as many points as did MEXICO in eight appearances.

WEST GERMANY, who did not enter the original tournament, was barred from entering in 1950. ITALY, who also chose to avoid the first World Cup, was prevented from competing in 1958 being knocked out of the qualifying group by NORTHERN IRELAND.

CANADA, DENMARK and IRAQ are competing for the first time.

7 WORLD CUP A–Z QUIZ

Test your World Cup knowledge – name the following:

A. The team that lost 2–4 in the Final of 1930.

B. England's goalkeeper in the 1966 Final.

C. He played for Holland in the 1974 Final.

D. Brazilian midfield star who played in the 1954, 1958 and 1962 World Cup competitions.

E. Portugal player much admired throughout Europe, who was the leading scorer in the 1966 competition.

F. English winger who kept the great Stanley Matthews out of the team on occasions, won a total of 76 caps and played in the World Cups of 1950 and 1954.

G. His real name was Manoel Francisco dos Santos. He was a winger who played in the 1958, 1962 and 1966 World Cups for Brazil, and he was perhaps the only player ever to have dribbling skills equal to those of Stanley Matthews.

H. They were drawn in the same group as Italy, Poland and Argentina in the 1974 World Cup and surprised everyone (especially the Italians!) by scoring first in their game against Italy.

I. Their match against Scotland during the 1978 tournament may have been the worst game ever played in a World Cup.

J. He played in the 1966, 1970 and 1974 World Cups, was a very effective winger and is the only man so far to score in each round of a competition – a feat he achieved in 1970.

K.   Dutch player who appeared in both the 1974 and 1978 World Cup Finals.

L.   One of the most gifted Scotland players of all time, who played only one game in the World Cup for his country.

M.   He played for Italy in the 1966, 1970 and 1974 World Cups and won 72 caps.

N.   Dutch midfield player who took part in the 1974 and 1978 World Cup finals and played for a time in Spain.

O.   A West German who took part in the 1966, 1970 and 1974 World Cups, he won a total of 81 caps as a midfield 'schemer'.

P.   His real name was Edson Arantes dos Nascimento, he played in four separate World Cup competitions, won over 100 caps and may be the best player of all time.

Q.   The surname of the quixotic character who kept goal for Peru in the 1978 and 1982 World Cups.

R.   An Italian who played in four World Cups. When dropped by his club side, he turned round and bought the club itself! A superbly-gifted midfield player.

S.   This country qualified to take part in the 1950 World Cup, but refused to play in a fit of pique!

T.   A Brazilian who played in the 1966 and 1970 competitions, whose real name was Eduardo Concalves de Andrade.

U.   A country which will be seeking its third victory in the tournament.

V.   Represented West Germany in the 1970, 1974 and 1978 World Cups.

W. He played in the 1950, 1954 and 1958 competitions and for a long time held the record of having played most times for England.

X. How successful a tipster are you? Attempt a prophecy at

The winner of the 1986 World Cup ....

The beaten Finalist ....

The beaten Semi-finalists ....

   and ....

Y. Played as a goalkeeper in the 1958, 1962 and 1966 World Cups.

Z. The oldest captain to gain the World Cup trophy.

Answers: Argentina, Banks, Cruyff, Didi, Eusebio, Finney, Garrincha, Haiti, Iran, Jairzinho, Krol, Law, Mazzola, Neeskens, Overath, Pelé, Quiroga, Rivera, Scotland, Tostao, Uruguay, Vogts, Wright, X, Yachin, Zoff.

8 THE TEAMS WHO HAVE QUALIFIED FOR MEXICO

A total of 121 teams entered the 1986 edition of the World Cup, playing in all 308 matches to see who would join Italy, the holders, and Mexico, the hosts. The first of these matches took place on 2 May 1984 between Cyprus and Austria and the last on 4 December 1985 between Australia – the winners of the Oceania Group – and Scotland.

Several well-established teams failed to see their way through the qualifying tournament. These included:

CZECHOSLOVAKIA (Finalist in 1934 and 1962)
HOLLAND (Finalist in 1974 and 1978)
SWEDEN (Finalist in 1958)
AUSTRIA (Semi-finalist in 1934 and 1954)
CHILE (Semi-finalist in 1962)
YUGOSLAVIA (Semi-finalist in 1930 and 1962)

Three teams are making their first appearance in a final tournament – CANADA, DENMARK and IRAQ – while 14 of those who qualified in 1982 have repeated the feat: ALGERIA, ARGENTINA, BELGIUM, BRAZIL, ENGLAND, FRANCE, HUNGARY, ITALY, NORTHERN IRELAND, POLAND, SCOTLAND, SPAIN, WEST GERMANY and USSR. BRAZIL were the only side from South America to qualify unbeaten while in Europe this claim could alone be made by ENGLAND. ALGERIA were the first side from Africa to qualify twice consecutively.

Three celebrated players hope to be making their fourth appearance. KENNY DALGLISH took part in all six of SCOTLAND'S games in 1974 and 1978 and appeared in two of the three games in 1982; UBALDO FILLOL appeared once for

ARGENTINA in 1974, four years later was goalkeeper to the side that won the World Cup and played in all five of his country's games in 1982; while WLADYSLAW ZMUDA has appeared at centre-back in all 20 of the games played by POLAND in the last three tournaments and seems well set to break the record of UWE SEELER for most appearances in the final stages of the World Cup (21).

This particular qualifying competition had its share of good and bad games. In the European Groups, the most astonishing day was undoubtedly 16 October 1985 when during the afternoon Northern Ireland played Rumania in Bucharest, winning thanks to a breakaway goal by Jimmy Quinn. The defence then had to suffer the most savage onslaught – but two men in particular proved equal to the task – the 40-year-old goalkeeper Pat Jennings, and the 23-year-old centre-back Alan McDonald, the latter winning his first cap but playing with all the assurance of one who had already gained years of experience. As if that result was not unexpected enough, in the evening Portugal gained entry to the final stages for the first time in 20 years by defeating West Germany in Stuttgart – the first occasion on which West Germany has ever lost a match in the qualifying competition and only five hours after Czechoslovakia had seen their hopes given new life after they had beaten the more-fancied Sweden in Prague. Carlos Manual it was who broke in from the left wing to rifle a crisp shot past Schumacher. And this only four days after Portugal had made desperately heavy weather of beating Malta 3–2 in Lisbon. France – as in 1977 and 1981 – did everything they could possibly do to keep doubts about their qualification extant until the very last game at home to Yugoslavia, which they had to win lest East Germany managed to secure a thumping victory against the already-qualified Bulgaria. In fact it managed to win 2–0; and in Group Six, although the Soviet Union started at snail's pace, taking only four points from its first five matches, the last three games produced six points. Denmark, however, headed the Group and could perform very well in Mexico. Suddenly – as with Holland 15 or so years ago – a crop of golden talent has been produced in that small country. Certainly the 4–2 victory for them

over the Soviet Union in Copenhagen in June 1985 was a match to
be savoured.

Another team of talent has appeared in Hungary (the first
European side to qualify), causing that country to enter the final
stages for the third consecutive time – ahead of the more-fancied
Austria and Holland. This last team, in fact, played in a play-off
against Belgium and were very optimistic, although they had lost
the first leg in Brussels by 1–0, since victory in the return game was
a distinct possibility. So it almost proved a month or so later as
Holland were in a 2–0 lead after 70 minutes and appeared to be
coasting to victory. It came, naturally – but not until after Georges
Grun had nipped in five minutes from the final whistle to score the
invaluable 'away' goal for Belgium that scuppered Holland's
chances. In Group Seven Wales let themselves down badly in their
first game, losing 1–0 to Iceland in Reykayvik. They then went on
to lose 3–0 to Spain away – and although they took seven points
from the remaining four games (which included a devastating 1–0
victory over Scotland in Glasgow and a 3–0 trouncing of Spain at
home) that last game against Scotland, in which victory was
imperative, only finished as a 1–1 draw, the Scotland goal coming
from a most harsh penalty. Rejoicing by Scotland that they still
remained in the competition was tarnished, however, by the death
soon after the game had finished of their enormously respected
manager, Jock Stein.

In South America the three countries 'expected' to qualify did
so, but not without several anxious moments. Uruguay were the
first team to qualify for the final stages and although Chile scored
first in the final match, a 2–1 victory went eventually to the home
team in Montevideo. Argentina also had its share of breathless
moments before managing finally to gain a 2–2 draw with Peru
who chose to field a midfield mastodon called Luis Reyna whose
marking of Diego Maradona made that of Gentile three years
earlier appear to resemble that 'of a gentleman'. Enough said.
Brazil proved to be the most sanguine qualifiers in this part of the
world thanks to having recalled all their stars who were earning
money in Italy, despite being managed by several different men, in
a muddle that continued until the very last (bringing back memor-

ies of 1970 when Mario Zagalo replaced Joao Saldanha with only
weeks to go); and it was no coincidence that the fourth qualifier
from South America (a repechage between all these teams who
had finished second, together with that which had finished third in
the larger group) was Paraguay who beat Colombia and Chile –
who, in turn, had defeated Peru, let down by some abysmal
goalkeeping.

Part of the reason for the expansion of the final stages to a total
of 24 teams lay in the desire of Joao Havelenge, the President of
FIFA (66 on 8 May) to make the World Cup reflect football as
played in all corners of the globe. Ask not what made the
authorities play off the winner of the Oceania section against a
European team (Australia lost to Scotland) but instead rejoice that
Canada at last have made it. I say 'at last' because in the qualifying
rounds of the previous tournament Canada almost qualified
before failing at the last hurdle. On this occasion, however, the
team gained an important victory in Tegucicalpa over Honduras
(who qualified for the previous tournament) which provided the
ideal springboard for victory. A notable triumph, this, seeing that
several of the players from Honduras have been playing in Spain.
During the month of June interest in Canada might even be
swayed from following those traditional sports such as baseball
and ice-hockey.

Algeria delighted many with the fluency of their football during
the 1982 World Cup – and should do so again. As should
Morocco, many of whose players are also based in France. South
Korea are a comparatively unknown quantity, having qualified for
the first time since 1954; but Italy, for one, is a country which will
look forward to their meeting with added interest, the name of Pak
Doo Ik (who scored the crucial goal when Italy were beaten 1–0 by
North Korea in the 1966 World Cup) being legendary throughout
Italy, and will watch closely the form of Choi Soon-Ho and of Cha
Bum-Kun, if he is recalled from West Germany where he has
been playing since 1979. Iraq, for its part, has a pair of redoubtable
centre-backs in Muthasar and Derjal and, having been coached by
three Brazilians, could provide some fascinating ideas in midfield
and attack.

In the following 20 pages we shall examine those teams who are competing but below is a brief table showing the six Groups at a glance. The seeded teams are shown with an asterisk.

GROUP A: *ITALY, BULGARIA, ARGENTINA, SOUTH KOREA
GROUP B: *MEXICO, BELGIUM, PARAGUAY, IRAQ
GROUP C: *FRANCE, CANADA, USSR, HUNGARY
GROUP D: *BRAZIL, SPAIN, ALGERIA, NORTHERN IRELAND
GROUP E: *WEST GERMANY, URUGUAY, SCOTLAND, DENMARK
GROUP F: *POLAND, MOROCCO, PORTUGAL, ENGLAND

Group A: Italy

Federazione Italiana Giuoco Calcio founded in 1898. Joined FIFA 1905.
   Previous appearances: 1934 (Winners), 1938 (Winners), 1950, 1954, 1962, 1966, 1970 (Finalists), 1974, 1978 (Fourth) and 1982 (Winners).
   Present tournament: Qualified automatically as Holders.
   The manager and players: ENZO BEARZOT (54) having guided Italy to the last two tournaments, remains in charge; the team was unbeaten during the 1984–5 season. GIOVANNI GALLI (28 on April 29) and FRANCO TANCREDI (31) are in contention for the position of goalkeeper but three other members of the defence are still in the team: ANTONIO CABRINI (28) as left-back, GAETANO SCIREA (33 on May 25) as *libero* and GIUSEPPE BERGOMI (22) as right-back with the speedy PIETRO VIERCHOWOD (27 on April 6) having taken over the role of stopper from FULVIO COL-LOVATI (29 on May 9) who will be in the party as may SEBAS-TIANO NELA (24), UBALDO RIGHETTI (23) and ROBERTO TRICELLA (27). The exciting SALVATORE BAGNI (29) now plays on the right-side of midfield, the playmaker of the team has recently been ANTONIO DI GENNARO (27) and MARCO TAR-DELLI (31) offers his great experience but there might be room for the defensive GIUSEPPE BARESI (27), the hard-working DANIELE MASSARO (25) – both of whom were in the Italian squad

in 1982 – as well as the stylish CARLO ANCELOTTI (26). BRUNO
CONTI (31) was one of the most exciting players in Spain, but
PIETRO FANNA (28 on June 23) has recently performed very well;
World Cups seem to bring the best out of the opportunist PAOLO
ROSSI (29). BRUNO GIORDANO is a most-gifted replacement,
SANDRO ALTOBELLI has been on very incisive form lately, as has
ALDO SERENA (26); and GIANLUCA VIALLI (21) has shown
himself to be the most gifted of the younger players.

Bulgaria

Federation Bulgare de Football founded in 1923. Joined FIFA in 1924.

Previous appearances: 1962, 1966, 1970 and 1974.

Present tournament: Finished Second in European Group 4 with 11
points from 8 games, behind FRANCE (0–1 away and 2–0 at home)
but in front of EAST GERMANY (1–0 at home, 1–2 away),
YUGOSLAVIA (0–0 away and 2–1 at home) and LUXEMBOURG
(4–0 at home and 3–1 away).

The manager and players: IVAN VUTZOV (46), who was Bulgaria's
centre-back during the 1966 World Cup, will be looking for his
country's first win in this competition but must have felt most
distressed by two events that occured a year ago within Bulgarian
football. First came a bribery scandal, which saw several officials being
sent to prison, and was followed – only weeks later – by a cup match
between CSKA Sofia and Levski Spartak that finished as a riot, as a
result of which several players were suspended for life, including some
from the national team. Now in goal will be ILIA VOLEV (25) with
BORISLOV MIKHAILOVICH as his stand-by; in front of them is a
trusted defence – KRASSIMIR KOEV (22), NICOLAI ARABOV
(32), GHEORGHI DMITROV (26) and PETAR PETROV (24).
ZIVKO GOSPODINOV (29) is one of the driving-forces in midfield
and will be aided by the experienced RADOSLAV ZDRAVKOV
(30), FYODOR ISKRENOV (26), ANJO SADAKOV (25) and
PLAMEN GUETOV (26). The star of the forward-line is undoubtedly STOICO MLADENOV (29) with also available BOJCO
VELICHKOV (28), RUSSI GOCHEV (27) or two players new to the
side, ATANAS PASHEV (22) and EDUARD ERANOSJIAN (24).
DIMITROV scored three of the 13 goals.

Argentina

Asociacion de Futbol Argentino founded in 1893. Joined FIFA in 1912.

Previous appearances: 1930 (Runners-up), 1934, 1958, 1962, 1966 (Quarter-finalists), 1974, 1978 (Winners) and 1982.

Present tournament: Headed South American Group 1 with 9 points from 6 games against PERU (0–1 away and 2–2 at home), COLOMBIA (3–1 away and 1–0 at home) and VENEZUELA (3–2 away and 3–0 at home).

The manager and players: CARLOS SALVADOR BILARDO, 47 and a doctor of medicine, succeeded CESAR LUIS MENOTTI as manager in may 1983 but his plans keep being rudely interrupted by the exodus of the most talented players to Europe. One such is the first-choice goalkeeper UBALDO FILLOL (36 on 21 July) whose deputies will be NERY PUMPIDO (28) and LUIS ISLAS (20) who has been selected only recently. NESTOR CLAUSEN (23) and OSCAR GARRE (29) are the first-choice fullbacks, the replacement being JULIAN CAMINO (25 on May 2). ENZO TROSSERO (33 on May 23) is the first-choice stopper, DANIEL PASSARELLA (33 on May 25) is the established sweeper with JOSE BROWN (29) and OSCAR RUGGERI (24) ready to take over in case of injury. The midfield can call upon the experienced RICARDO BOCHINI (32), JUAN BARBAS (26), MIGUEL RUSSO (30 on April 9), RICARDO GIUSTI (29) as well as JORGE BURRUCHUGA (23) and DIEGO ARMANDO MARADONA (25) who link up with the attack. There we have OSCAR DERTYCIA (21), RICARDO GARECA (28) and CLAUDIO DANIEL BORGHI (21) along with three who are playing in Europe – PEDRO PASCULLI (26 on May 17) and RAMON DIAZ (26) who are playing in Italy, and JORGE VALDANO (30), presently with Real Madrid. MARADONA and PASCULLI both scored 3 goals in the Qualifying Round, PASSARELLA 2; and ARGENTINA should go far in this tournament. When you are blessed with a genius such as MARADONA, anything is possible.

South Korea

Football Association founded 1928. Joined FIFA in 1948.

Previous appearance: 1954 (beaten 9–0 by Hungary and 7–0 by Turkey).

Present tournament: Won sub-Group over NEPAL (4–0 at home, 2–0 away) and MALAYSIA (0–1 away, 2–0 at home) then in semi-final beat INDONESIA (2–0 at home, 4–1 away) and in final beat Japan (2–1 away, 1–0 at home).

The manager and players: KIM CHUNG-NAM (42), often referred to as 'Lucky Kim', on account of the good fortune he has often experienced as a ruthless sweeper, is now an even more ruthless manager. CHO BYUNG-DUK (28 on May 26) is the first-choice goalkeeper with OH YUN-KYO (26 on May 25) as his deputy and CHO KIN-KOOK (23 on July 5) as first-choice sweeper, YOO BYUNG-OK (22) being in reserve. PARK KYUNG-HOON (25), JUNG YONG-HWAN (26), KIM PYUNG-SUK (27) and CHO YOUNG-JEUNG (31) are other experienced defenders. CHO KWANG-RAE (32) and PARK CHANG-SUN (32) organise the midfield with the free-scoring HUH JUNG-MOO (31) or LEE TAE-HO (25) alongside. CHOI SOON-HO (24) is the stylish centre-forward playing between KIM JONG-BOO (21) on his right and KIM SOO-SUNG (20) on his left and there is always CHA BUM-KUN (33 on May 25) to call on although he didn't feature in any of the qualifying games on account of his being required in West German club football, where he has been playing for several seasons. Of the 17 goals scored by South Korea in the qualifying round, four came from HUH JUNG-MOO but almost every one of the younger players from South Korea will be seeking to impress coaches in other parts of the world.

Group B: Mexico

Mexican Football Association founded in 1927. Joined FIFA in 1929.

Previous appearances: 1930, 1950, 1954, 1958, 1962, 1966, 1970 (Quarter-Finalists) and 1978.

Present tournament: Qualified automatically as hosts.

The manager and players: VELIBOR (BORA) MILUTINOVIC (7 September 1944) is a Yugoslav who, after playing in his home country and France, moved on to the Mexican side Universidad Nacional (UNAM). After he retired in 1975 he was appointed club coach, guiding the team to several successes, and in 1982 was named national coach. He thinks that Mexican football is in between what he defines

as 'the improvisation' of Latin football and the disciplined football of
teams such as West Germany, the Soviet Union and England and has
been attempting to meld together the finer points of the individual and
collective game. One factor, of course, very much in the favour of the
host side is the particular climate, for Mexican players will not have to
spend time becoming acclimatised. In goal will be PABLO LARIOS
(25) with CARLOS OLAF HEREDIA (28) as his deputy; at right-
back MARCO ALBERTO TREJO (30), FELIX BARBOSA (25 on
April 4), ARMANDO MANZO (27), FERNANDO QUIRARTE
GUTTIEREZ (30 on May 17), and left-back RAFAEL AMADOR
(27) or RAUL SERVIN MONETTI (23 on April 29). Alfredo Tena
(29), an experienced central defender, was in the party for the 1978
World Cup. The midfield should be made up by MANUEL NEG-
RETE (26), CARLOS MUNOZ (25), MIGUEL ESPANA (22),
CARLOS DE LOS COBOS (27), ALEJANDRO DOMINGUEZ
(24), with JAVIER AGUIRRE (27), TOMAS BOY (34 on June 28)
and FRANCISCO CHAVEZ (26), all of whom like to join the attack
in which feature CARLOS HERMOSILLO (25), LUIS FLORES
(24) as well as the undoubted star of the team, HUGO SANCHEZ
(27), who plays for Real Madrid.

Belgium

*Union Royale Belge des Societes de Football Association founded in 1895.
Joined FIFA in 1904.*

Previous appearances: 1930, 1934, 1938, 1954, 1970 and 1982.

Present tournament: Second in European Group 1 with 8 points from
6 games against POLAND (2–0 at home and 0–0 away), ALBANIA
(3–1 at home and 0–2 away) and GREECE (0–0 away and 2–0 at
home). Then defeated HOLLAND (1–0 at home and 1–2 away in the
play-off repechage against the team that finished second in European
Group 5).

The manager and players: GUY THYS (63) was appointed manager
in August 1977 and steered his side to the European Championships
of 1980 (when they were Finalists). Several of the players who played
in Spain are still available. The much-respected JEAN-MARIE
PFAFF (33 on April 12) is playing now in West Germany for Bayern
Munchen and has JACQUES MUNARON (29) as his able deputy.

ERIC GERETS (32 on May 18) has re-established himself as right-back; HUGO BROOS (34 on April 10) has emerged as the left-back; and FRANKY VAN DER ELST (25 on April 30), MICHEL RENQUIN (30), GEORGES GRUN (24) and MICHEL DE WOLF (28) have also played recently. The new star of the team is VICENZO SCIFO (20), who was first selected in 1984, but around him are players of experience – FRANKIE VERCAUTEREN (29), RENÉ VANDEREYCKEN (32), and JAN CEULEMANS (29) who now plays deeper. ERWIN VANDENBERGH (27), ALEX CZERNIATYNSKI (25), PHILIPPE DESMET (23), EDDY VOODECKERS (26) and NICO CLAESAN (23) are forwards who played in the qualifying round. FRANKIE VERCAUTEREN scored three of the nine goals scored.

Paraguay

Association founded in 1906. Joined FIFA in 1921.

Previous appearances: 1930, 1950, 1958.

Present tournament: Finished Second in South American Group 3 behind BRAZIL (0–2 at home and 1–1 away) but in front of BOLIVIA (1–1 away and 3–0 at home). Won the play-off Group against COLOMBIA (3–0 at home and 1–2 away) and CHILE (3–0 at home and 2–2 away).

The manager and players: CAYETANO RE (52), who played inside-forward when Paraguay last competed in the World Cup Finals 28 years ago, nearly resigned as manager after Paraguay had at last qualified, complaining that since so many key players featured for clubs in other countries he would be unable to weld together an effective unit. Nevertheless, no team that wins both home matches at the play-off stage 3–0 should be taken lightly. ROBERTO 'GATO' FERNANDEZ (31) played in the play-off matches and EVER ALMEIDA (28) in the Group matches from the qualifying Group and in front of them is a defence of PEDRO TORALES (27), ROGELIO DELGADO (25) – who is a very tight marker, CESAR ZAVALA (26) and CESAR SCHIATTINA (25). The star of the team undoubtedly is JULIO CESAR ROMERO (26) who plays in Brazil, while JORGE NUNES (27) and BUENAVENTURA FERREIRA (28) play for teams in Colombia, and GUSTAVO BENITEZ (28), has played in

Spain. ADOLFINO CANETE (24) is a very talented goal-maker; ROBERTO CABANAS (27) has experience of playing for Cosmos in the USA; and EMILIANO HICKS (24) is a fast-moving winger. ROMERO was the chief scorer with four of the 12 goals.

Iraq

Iraqui Football Association founded in 1948. Joined FIFA in 1951.

Previous appearances: None.

Present tournament: Winner of an Asian place against JORDAN (3–2 away and 2–0 at home), UNITED ARAB EMIRATES (3–2 away and 1–2 at home, qualifying thanks to away goals) and SYRIA (0–0 away and 3–1 at home).

The manager and players: The Brazilian JORGE SILVA DE VIERA (52) has as his assistants EDUARDO ANTUNES COIMBRA (39), the brother of ZICO, who briefly two years ago was manager to Brazil, and CARLOS ALBERTO LANCETTA (42) as the trainer. Since there are few more than 3,000 registered players in Iraq, qualification for the World Cup Finals represents a tremendous triumph but in the past few years the team has gained victories in the Gulf Championship, the Arab Olympics and the Asian Olympics (1984) in addition to reaching the final stages of the two last complete Olympic Games in Moscow and Los Angeles (when the team drew 1–1 with CANADA). Many of the players are members of the club side Az-Zawraa of Baghdad. RAAD HAMMOUDI (30) will be in goal and GHANIM UREIBI (24) at right-back; KHALID ALLAWI (23) is a goal-scoring left-back while there is much experience in the centre of the defence, KHADIM MUTASHAR (29) being a powerful stopper and ADNAN DIRJAL (30) a very gifted sweeper. In midfield will be SHAKIR MAHMOUD (26), BASIL GEORGIS (24) and HARIS MUHAMMAD (23), while in attack should be ALI HUSSEIN (22), AHMAD RADHI (25) and HUSSEIN SAID (24) who scored four times in the qualifying tournament.

Group C: France

Federation Francaise de Football founded 1919. Joined FIFA 1904.

Previous appearances: 1930, 1934, 1938, 1958 (Third), 1966, 1978 and 1982 (Fourth).

Present tournament: Headed European Group 4 with 11 points from 8 games ahead of BULGARIA (0–2 away and 1–0 at home), EAST GERMANY (2–0 at home and 0–2 away), YUGOSLAVIA (0–0 away and 2–0 at home) and LUXEMBOURG (4–0 away and 6–0 at home).

The manager and players: HENRI MICHEL (38) succeeded MICHEL HILDAGO whose eight-year reign as the French manager culminated with France winning the 1984 edition of the European Championship, having himself steered France to victory in the 1984 Olympic Games. JOEL BATS (29) has established himself as first-choice goalkeeper, ALBERT RUST (32) being his stand-by. WILLIAM AYACHE (25) is a young right-back of great promise; MANUEL AMOROS (24) has been selected frequently; and JEAN-FRANCOIS DOMERQUE (29 on June 23) has been chosen regularly at left-back. YVON LE ROUX (26 on April 19) has made the position of stopper his own and the role of sweeper will be filled by either PATRICK BATTISTON (29) or MAXIME BOSSIS (31 on June 26). There is a wealth of talent in midfield which has been built around the special skills of MICHEL PLATINI (31 on June 21) and the diminutive ALAIN GIRESSE (33). LUIS FERNANDEZ (26) shone in the European Championships; JEAN TIGANA (31 on June 23) is a regular player as is BERNARD GENGHINI (28), and JEAN-MARC FERRARI (23) is a fresh face of great talent. DOMINIQUE ROCHETEAU (31) has been on very incisive form in the attack; JOSÉ TOURE (25 on April 24) has featured regularly alongside him, and also available should be BRUNO BELLONE (24) YANNICK STOPYRA (25) and the Belgian based JEAN-PIERRE PAPIN (22) who made an excellent début against Northern Ireland on 26 February 1986. PLATINI was the highest scorer with four goals, ROCHETEAU and STOPYRA following him with three each.

Canada

Canadian Football Association founded in 1912. Joined FIFA in 1948.

Previous appearances: None.

Present tournament: Qualified for the only CONCACAF place by beating (First Round) JAMAICA (Walkover), (Second Round) HAITI (2–0 at home and 2–0 away) and GUATEMALA (2–1 at home and 1–1 away) and (Third Round) HONDURAS (1–0 away and 2–1 at home) and COSTA RICA (1–1 at home and 0–0 away).

The manager and players: TONY WAITERS (48), a former international goalkeeper for England in 1964/5, came to Canada in 1977 in order to coach Vancouver Whitecaps with whom he stayed until 1982. He has the proud honour of having steered Canada to the finals of the World Cup for the very first time – this despite the discouraging collapse of the game in the USA during 1985. TINO LETTIERI (28) is the first-choice goalkeeper with the tall SVEN HABERMANN (24) among the reserves. The experienced BRUCE WILSON (35 on June 20) is at right-back, with BOB LENARDUZZI (31 on May 1), RANDY SAMUEL (22), TREVOR McCALLUM (22) or IAN BRIDGE (26) taking the places in the centre of the defence, and at left-back TERRY MOORE (28 on June 2), who has experience of playing in Europe. In midfield should be DAVID NORMAN (24 on May 6), RANDY RAGAN (27), MIKE SWEENEY (25), GREG ION (23) or PAUL JAMES (22) who has experience of playing for Newport County. Among the forwards will be DALE MITCHELL (26), BRANKO SEGOTA (25 on June 8), IGOR VRABLIC (20), in addition to CARL VALENTINE (28 on July 4) who has experience of playing in the English First Division.

USSR

Federation founded 1912. Joined FIFA 1946.

Previous appearances: 1958 (Quarter-finalists), 1962 (Quarter-finalists), 1966 (Fourth), 1970 (Quarter-finalists) and 1982.

The present tournament: Finished second in European Group 6 with 10 points from 8 matches behind DENMARK (2–4 away and 1–0 at home) but ahead of SWITZERLAND (2–2 away and 4–0 at home), REPUBLIC OF IRELAND (0–1 away and 2–0 at home) and NORWAY (1–1 away and 1–0 at home).

The manager and players: EDUARD MALAFEEV (44 on June 10), who played at inside-forward for the Soviet Union in the 1966 World Cup, was appointed manager in May 1984 after he had steered Dynamo Minsk to winning the League championship and his country had disappointingly failed to qualify for the finals of the European Championships. The outstanding RENAT DASSAEV (29 on April 12) is still in goal and two other players who were taken to Spain, ANATOLY DEMIANENKO (27) and the elegant *libero* ALEXANDR CHIVADZE (31 on April 8), have also been included. Successful as the right-back has been GENNADI MOROZOV (33) while ALEKSANDR BUBNOV (26) has been a most authoritative stopper, with SERGEI BALATCHA (27) among the reserves. FEODOR CHERENKOV (26) has made astonishing progress as the schemer of the team and others who have played in midfield include the experienced VLADIMIR BESSONOV (28), ANDREI ZYC-MANTOVICH (23), GENNADI LIVTOCHENKO (22), and ALEKSANDR ZAVAROV (25 on April 26). SERGEI GOTS-MANOV (27 on March 27) is a midfield player who is very strong on the counter-attack, OLEG BLOKHIN (33) is still capable of troubling most defences and accompanying him will be the new sensation OLEG PROTASOV (22) who scored five of the 13 Soviet goals in the Qualifying Rounds. Among the reserves are GEORGI KONDRATIEV (26) and SERGEI RODIONOV (23).

Hungary

Magyar Labdarugok Szovetsege founded in 1901. Joined FIFA in 1907.

Previous appearances: 1934, 1938 (Finalists), 1954 (Finalists), 1958, 1962 (Quarter-finalists), 1966 (Quarter-finalists), 1978 and 1982.

Present tournament: Headed European Group 5 with 10 pts from 6 games over HOLLAND (2–1 away and 0–1 at home), AUSTRIA (3–1 at home and 3–0 away) and CYPRUS (2–1 away and 2–0 at home).

The manager and players: GYORGY MEZEY (45 on September 7) who was appointed manager in July 1983, was formerly in charge of the Olympic team and has made significant changes in the personnel of the squad. PETER DISZTL (26) has become the first-choice goalkeeper, his reserves being JOZSEF ANDRUSCH (30) and JOZSEF SZENDREI (32) while the defence has been formed by SANDOR SALLAI (26), ANTAL ROTH (25), the experienced

ANTAL NAGY (29) and ZOLTAN PETER (28) with JOZSEF VARGA (26), presently playing in Turkey, and LASZLO DISTL (26) among the reserves. The midfield has been made up by the very experienced IMRE GARABA (28), the highly gifted LAJOS DETARI (23 on April 24), JOZSEF KARDOS (26) and the renowned TIBOR NYILASI (30), a deep-lying centre-forward who now plays for Austria Vienna. The most favoured forwards have been JOZSEF KIPRICH (22), MARTON EZTERHAZY (30 on April 9), who plays in Greece, KALMAN KOVACS (20), BELA BODONYI (29) and, although he has not been selected for several matches, there might still be room for the mercurial ANDRAS TOROCYZYK (31 on May 1) who is now playing in France. EZTERHAZY, DETARI, NIYALSI and KIPRICH each scored 2 of the 12 Hungarian goals.

Group D: Brazil

Confederacao Brasileira do Futebol founded in 1914. Joined FIFA in 1923.

Previous appearances: 1930, 1934, 1938 (Third), 1950 (Finalists), 1954 (Quarter-finalists), 1958 (Winners), 1962 (Winners), 1966, 1970 (Winners), 1974 (Fourth), 1978 (Third), 1982.

Present tournament: Headed South American Group 3 with 6 points from 4 matches against PARAGUAY (2–0 away and 1–1 at home) and BOLIVIA (2–0 away and 1–1 at home).

The manager and players: Since the 1982 World Cup, several Brazilian managers have come and gone but it was TELE SANTANA (manager of the side in Spain) who guided the team through its qualifying Group. This lack of stability has not helped the formation of a settled side but the men who saw Brazil through the qualifying round were CARLOS (30) in goal and in front of him a defence that read LEANDRO (27), OSCAR (32 on June 20), EDINHO (31 on June 5) and JUNIOR (32 on June 19). In midfield were SOCRATES (32), ZICO (33) and CEREZO (31), while among the forwards were RENATO GAUCHO (27), CASAGRANDE (23 on April 15) who scored three of Brazil's six goals, CARECA (25) and EDER (29 on May 25), complete with his electrifying free-kicks. Also in contention might be one of the 'old guard' – PAULO ROBERTO FALCAO (32) – while among fresh talent is the highly-gifted GEOVANI SILVA (24 on April 6), EDSON (26), ALEMEO (24), MARINHO (23) – a young black winger who is being compared to the immortal

Garrincha – together with MOZER (25) and DIDA (24) in defence, and in the forwards the gifted MULLER (22), SILAS (20) and FIDNEY (22) who are now starting to play to their full potential.

Spain

Real Federacion Espanola de Futbol founded 1913. Joined FIFA 1904.

Previous appearances: 1934 (Quarter-finalists), 1950 (Fourth), 1962, 1966, 1978 and 1982.

Present tournament: Headed European Group 7 with 8 points from 6 games against SCOTLAND (1–3 away and 1–0 at home), WALES (3–0 at home and 0–3 away) and ICELAND (2–1 away and 2–1 at home).

The manager and players: MIGUEL MUNOZ (64 on January 19) took charge soon after the departure of the former manager, JOSÉ SANTAMARIA, who was unable to provide the desired result (a third consecutive 'home' victory) four years ago. But Spain did reach the final of the 1984 European Nations Championship and although the passage through the qualifying Group did have its share of anxious moments (notably the defeat by the luckless WALES) Munoz has built a team of some talent. In goal will be ANDONI ZUBI-ZARETTA (24), LUIS ARCONADA (32 on June 26) or FRAN-CISCO BUYO (28) and the defence should be drawn from MIRAN-DA GERARDO (26), the hard-tackling ANDONI GOIECOCHEA (27), the tall, blond sweeper ANTONIO MACEDA (29), the vastly-experienced JOSÉ CAMACHO (31) or JULIO ALBERTO (27) – a right-back who likes to help mount attacks. The midfield is built around the skills of RAFAEL GORDILLO (31), a former left-back who likes to drive through setting up attacks, RICARDO GALLEGO (28 on May 11), MIGUEL MICHEL (23) who has a fearsome shot and VICTOR MUNOZ (29), with FRANCISCO JAVIER LOPEZ (23) being the most outstanding of the reserves. In the attack the star undoubtedly is EMILIO BUTRAGUENO (22) who plays his club football alongside Jorge Valdano of Argentina and Hugo Sanchez of Mexico. Aiding and abetting him in the scoring of goals will be HIPOLITO RINCON (29), the heading power of CARLOS SANTILLANA (33), with service coming from either the speedy FRANCISCO CARRASCO (27), JUAN ROJO (25), or the recent discovery ELOY (22) on the wings.

Algeria

Federation Algerienne de Football founded 1962. Joined FIFA 1963.

Previous appearance: 1982.

Present tournament: Beat ANGOLA (0–0 away and 3–2 at home), ZAMBIA (2–0 at home and 1–0 away) and TUNISIA (4–1 away and 3–0 at home).

The manager and players: RABAH SADAANE (41), who assumed the position of coach to the national team at the beginning of 1985, is fortunate in being able to call on many of the players who delighted in Spain four years ago. Several of them have featured in European leagues (France, Belgium, Portugal and Switzerland) and have gained valuable experience of top-class football. NASR-EDIENNE DRID (25) has become first-choice goalkeeper ahead of MEHDI CERBAH (33) who played in Spain. ABDALLAH LIEGEON (28) is now the right-back; MAHMOUD GENDOUZ (33) is sweeper; the stopper is the tall NORREDINE KOURICHI (32 on April 12); and at left-back is FAOUZI MANSOURI (30) – a very tight marker, HAMID SADMI (24) being among the reserves. In midfield the choice is abundant. FAISAL MEGUENNI (20 on June 28) is a young player of great talent and will vie with KARIM MAROC (30), MOHAMED KACI-SAID (28 on May 2), TADJ BENSAOULA (31), ALI FERGANI (33) or DJAMEL JAFJAF (22), to play alongside the star of the side, LAKHDAR BELLOUMI (27). In the attack will be RABAH MADJER (28), SALAH ASSAD (27), DANIEL ZIDANE (31 on May 22), all of whom have played frequently, or DJAMEL MENAD (25) and NASSER BOUICHE (26), both newcomers full of courage and determination who have been scoring regularly. Well organised and full of players who have solid experience, Algeria could cause a few surprises in June.

Northern Ireland

Irish Football Association founded 1880. Joined FIFA 1911–1920, 1924–28, 1946.

Previous appearances: 1958 (Quarter-finalists), 1982.

Present tournament: Second in European Group 3 with 10 points from 8 games behind ENGLAND (0–1 at home and 0–0 away) but in front of RUMANIA (3–2 at home and 1–0 away), FINLAND (0–1 away and 2–1 at home), and TURKEY (2–0 at home and 0–0 away).

The manager and players: BILLY BINGHAM, 55, has first-hand experience of the World Cup since he was a member of the team that performed with such zest in 1958. Indeed, the astonishing displays in the World Cup of 1982 – during which the team defeated the host country, Spain, and reached the Second Round – brought back fond memories of that earlier triumph, against all forecasts. In this qualifying round, Northern Ireland carried on with the tradition of providing the unexpected by doing what England couldn't do: defeating Rumania twice. In goal is still the magnificent PAT JENNINGS (41 on June 12), JIM PLATT (37) being his replacement. JIMMY NICHOLL (29) is still at right-back, but the fearless ALAN McDONALD (25) has come in to bolster the centre of the defence which might include JOHN O'NEILL (31) and JOHN McCLELLAND (29) and has MAL DONAGHY at left-back. The midfield is rich with talent, having NIGEL WORTHINGTON (24) coming into contention alongside SAMMY McILROY (31), DAVID McCREERY (28), MARTIN O'NEILL (34) – if he recovers from injury – and NORMAN WHITESIDE (21 on May 7). There is much experience in the forward-line with GERRY ARMSTRONG (32 on May 23), BILLY HAMILTON (29 on May 9), the extrovert IAN STEWART (24) and NOEL BROTHERSTON (29) being joined by JIMMY QUINN (25) and COLIN CLARKE (23). Of the eight goals scored by Northern Ireland NORMAN WHITESIDE scored three.

Group E: West Germany

Deutscher Fussball-Bund founded in 1900. Joined FIFA in 1904–1945, 1950.

Previous appearances (including pre-war Germany): 1934 (Third), 1938, 1954 (Winners), 1958 (Fourth), 1962 (Quarter-finalists), 1966 (Finalists), 1970 (Third), 1974 (Winners), 1978 and 1982 (Finalists).

Present tournament: Headed European Group 2 with 12 points from 8 games against PORTUGAL (2–1 away and 0–1 home), SWEDEN (2–0 at home and 2–2 away), CZECHOSLOVAKIA (5–1 away and 2–2 at home) and MALTA (3–2 away and 6–0 at home).

The manager and players: FRANZ BECKENBAUER (40), who

succeeded JUPP DERWALL after the disappointing displays in the
1984 European Nations Championship, must have been delighted by
that 5–1 victory in Prague on 1 May 1985. That, however, was the last
of the pleasant news, since the defeat by Portugal came in the middle
of a run of 10 consecutive games without a victory. HARALD
SCHUMACHER (32) is still the first-choice goalkeeper. THOMAS
BERTHOLD (21) and MICHAEL FRONTZECK (22) are the
fullbacks, KARL-HEINZ FORSTER (27) and KLAUS AU-
GENTHALER (28) are at the centre of the defence but ANDREAS
BREHME (25) and DITMAR JAKOBS (32) have also played.
OLAF THON (20 on May 1) and UWE RAHN (24 on May 21) were
brought into midfield and played brilliantly for a while but BECKEN-
BAUER may opt for 'experienced' people such as WOLFGANG
ROLFF (25), HANS-PETER BRIEGEL (30), the link between the
defence and midfield as can be the talented MATTHIAS HERGET
(30), FELIX MAGATH (33 on July 26) and LOTHAR MATTH-
AUS (25) but the wonderfully-gifted BERND SCHUSTER (26)
may be the key. Among the forwards have been KLAUS ALLOFS
(29), PIERRE LITTBARSKI (26 on April 16), RUDI VOLLER (26
on APRIL 13) and the gifted KARL-HEINZ RUMMENIGGE (30)
who scored 4 of the 22 West German goals, KLAUS ALLOFS,
LITTBARSKI and UWE RAHN scoring 3 each. Sadly, both Rahn
and Voller might miss the finals on account of injury.

Uruguay

Football Associacion founded in 1900. Joined FIFA in 1923.

   Previous appearances: 1930 (Winners), 1950 (Winners), 1954
(Semi-finalists), 1968, 1966 (Quarter-finalists), 1970 (Semi-finalists)
and 1974.

   Present tournament: Headed South American Group 2 with 6 points
from 4 games against CHILE (0–2 away and 2–1 at home) and
ECUADOR (2–1 at home and 2–0 away).

   The manager and players: OMAR BORRAS (55) was appointed
manager in February 1982, since when his team has triumphed in
every cup competition that it has entered. The first-choice goalkeeper
has for almost the last decade been RODOLFO RODRIGUEZ (30)
with FERNANDO ALVEZ (25) as his stand-by. The backs will be
drawn from NESTOR MONTELONGO (31), NELSON
GUTIERREZ (24), EDUARDO ACEVADEO (26), DARIO

PEREYRA (30), VICTOR DIOGO (26) and JOSÉ BATISTA (24),
but if Borras feels uneasy about his defence he might call on the
'services' of HUGO DE LEON (28) who has been playing in Brazil
for several seasons. Sealing up the midfield will be MIGUEL BOS-
SIO (26), MARIO SARALEGUI (27), SERGIO SANTIN (26) and
the experienced JORGE BARRIOS (25) while the jewel of the side,
the free-scoring ENZO FRANCESCOLI (25), seeks to make bullets
for the attack whose principal figures should be the recent discovery
CARLOS AGUILERA (22), in addition to those imported from
Spain – WILMAR CABRERA (27 on July 31), JORGE DA SILVA
(24) – and VENANCIO RAMOS (27 on June 20) who has been
playing in France and was the leading scorer in the qualifying round
with two of the six goals. Uruguay will certainly be a difficult side to
beat and as long as they don't needlessly waste their energies and
harness their aggression the players are quite capable of going all the
way.

Scotland

*Scottish Football Association founded in 1873. Joined FIFA 1910–20,
1924–28, 1946.*

   Previous tournaments: 1954, 1958, 1974, 1978 and 1982.

   Present tournament: Finished Second in European Group 7 with 7
points from 6 games behind SPAIN (3–0 at home and 0–1 away) but
in front of WALES (0–1 at home and 1–1 away) and ICELAND (3–0
at home and 1–0 away). Then beat AUSTRALIA in play-off game
(2–0 at home and 0–0 away).

   The manager and players: ALEX FERGUSON (46) was assistant to
JOCK STEIN and succeeded him after the latter's tragic death
moments following that 1–1 draw in Cardiff and was in charge of the
team for those two games against Australia. In the second of those,
JIM LEIGHTON (27) had a wonderfully sure match, giving confidence to the men in front of him who included his club-colleagues at
Aberdeen, WILLIE MILLER (31 on May 2) and ALEX McLEISH
(27) DAVID NAREY (30 on May 6) being chief reserve in the centre
of the defence. STEVE NICOL (24) has come in as a strong-running
right-back, and the left-back place has been filled by either
MAURICE MALPAS (26) or ARTHUR ALBISTON (28).
GRAEME SOUNESS (33 on May 6) organises the midfield with

alongside him JIM BETT (25), PAUL McSTAY (20), MURDO MCLEOD (26), ROY AITKEN (27) and GORDON STRACHAN (29). In attack may be STEVE ARCHIBALD (29) who has been scoring freely for Barcelona for the last two seasons, MO JOHN-STON (23), the inspiring KENNY DALGLISH (35), DAVID COOPER (29), GRAEME SHARP (25) or the prolific FRANK McAVENNIE (26) and surely there must be room for the prodigious talents of CHARLIE NICHOLAS (24)?

Denmark

Federation Dansk Boldspil-Union founded 1889. Joined FIFA 1904.

Previous appearances: None.

Present tournament: Headed European Group 6 with 11 points from 8 games against SOVIET UNION (4–2 at home, 0–1 away), SWITZERLAND (0–1 away and 0–0 at home), REPUBLIC OF IRELAND (3–0 at home and 4–1 away) and NORWAY (1–0 at home and 5–1 away).

The manager and players: Much of the advance of Danish football in recent years is due to the rigorous regime introduced by SEPP PIONTEK (46) since he became national coach in 1979. Indeed, Denmark seems to enjoy following the exploits of a large clutch of talented players, and could prove to be the most successful team taking part in the competition for the first time since Portugal 20 years earlier. In goal should be OLE QUIST (36) or the younger TROELS RASMUSSEN (25); JOHN SIVEBECK (25) is a right-back who loves to attack; SOREN BUSK (33 on April 10) is a rigorous stopper who has much experience of playing alongside MORTEN OLSEN (36) the accomplished libero of the side, with IVAN NIELSEN (29) being the regular left-back. JAN MOLBY (23 on July 4) can use his skills in defence but if chosen in midfield will play alongside KLAUS BERGGREN (27), FRANK ARNESEN (29), JOHN BERTLSEN (34), JOHN LAURITSEN (27) and SOREN LERBY (28). In the attack there is JESPER OLSEN (25 on March 20); on the right-wing, PREBEN EKLJAER-LARSEN (28), the young, blond MICHEL LAUDRUP (21), and ALLAN SIMONSEN (33) being the much-capped campaigner. ELKJAER scored eight of the 17 goals, the highest number scored by anyone in the qualifying tournament, four coming from LAUDRUP.

Group F: Poland

Polski Zwiazek Pilki Niznej (PZPN) founded in 1919. Joined FIFA 1923.
   Previous appearances: 1938, 1974 (Third), 1978 and 1982 (Third).
   Present tournament: Headed European Group 1 over BELGIUM
(0–2 away and 0–0 at home), ALBANIA (2–2 at home and 1–0 away)
and GREECE 3–1 at home and 4–1 away).
   The manager and players: ANTONI PIECHNIZEK (45) was
appointed manager in January 1981 and speedily blended in promising new talent with older, more mature players. Several who performed so well four years ago in Spain are still in the team. JOSEF
MYLNARCZYK (32) is one of the most accomplished goalkeepers in
circulation, recently has played in France and is now with Porto in
Portugal. MAREK OSTROWSKI (26) and KRZYSZTOF PAW-
LAK (28) are a pair of experienced fullbacks and ROMAN WO-
JCICKI (28), KAZIMIERZ PRZYBYS (26 on July 11) together with
the extremely experienced WLADYSLAW ZMUDA (32 on June 6)
make a central defence that is the equal of any in the world. ZBIG-
NIEW BONIEK (30) is a world-famous midfield player and along-
side him will be WALDEMAR MATYSIK (24), JAN URBAN (24
on May 14), the elegant RYSZARD KOMORNICKI (26),
ANDRZEJ BUNCOL (26), although he has experienced a tragic loss
of form since he delighted everyone in Spain, or KRZYSTOF
BARAN (26 on July 26) who had the most astonishing debut for his
country, scoring both goals in the 2–2 draw with Uruguay in Montevideo during February. Among the strikers will be the experienced
WLODZIMIERZ SMOLAREK (28), ANDRZEJ PALASZ (26 on
July 22), MIROSLAW OKONSKI (27), ANDRZEJ IWAN (26),
who was in the party for both Argentina and Spain, and the new star of
Polish football, DARIUSZ DZIEKANOWSKI (23). Of the 10 goals
scored by Poland SMOLAREK and DZIEKANOWSKI scored 3
each.

Morocco

Moroccan Football Association founded 1955. Joined FIFA 1956.
   Previous appearance: 1970. (Lost 1–2 to WEST GERMANY and
0–3 to PERU but drew 1–1 with BULGARIA.)
   Present tournament: Beat SIERRA LEONE (1–0 away and 4–0 at

home), MALAWI (2–0 at home and 0–0 away), EGYPT (0–0 away and 2–0 at home) and LIBYA (3–0 at home and 0–1 away).

The manager and players: The Brasilian JOSÉ FARIA (52) is the man who has been overseeing the fortunes of Moroccan footballers over the past few seasons – and it is no surprise that this has lead to a system in which a 4–4–2 system changes rapidly into 4–2–4. The goalkeeper is the acrobatic EZAKI BADOU (27 on April 2) – known better as 'ZAKI' – who has in front of him HAMMOU FADILI (28) on the right, NOUREDINE BOUYAHYAOUI (31) as an accomplished sweeper, MUSTAPHA EL BIAZ (25) as stopper and ABDELMAJID LAMRISS (27) as left back – in reserve being MUSTAPHA BIDANE (20), LAHCEN OUDANI (26) and MUSTAPHA FIDADI (23 on May 23). The midfield should be the strong point of the side presenting ABDELMAJID DOLMY (33 on April 19), MUSTAPHA EL HADDAOUI (30), the goal-scoring AZIZ BOUDERBALA (26) – both of whom play in Switzerland – and the highly-talented MOHAMED TIMOUMI (26) who is known as the 'African Pele'. In the attack are KHALID EL BIEDKOV (29), ABDELLATIF RHIATI (23) while playing in France are the MERRY brothers, ABDELKARIN (known better as KRIMAU) (31) who has been scoring regularly for his club side of Le Havre, and MUSTAPHA (28 on April 21).

Portugal

Federacio Federcalcao Portuguesa de Futebol founded 1914. Joined FIFA 1926.

Previous appearance: 1966 (Third).

Present tournament: Qualified Second in European Group 2 with 10 points from 8 games behind WEST GERMANY (1–2 at home and 1–0 away) but in front of SWEDEN (1–0 away and 1–3 at home), CZECHOSLOVAKIA (2–1 at home and 0–1 away) and MALTA (3–1 away and 3–2 at home).

The manager and players: Victory in Sweden only to be beaten in the return match, a loss at home to Germany only to record later a historic victory in Stuttgart – and this only four days after the team had struggled to beat Malta in Lisbon. Overseeing this catalogue of upsets was JOSÉ TORRES (47) whom many will remember for leading his country's attack in the 1966 World Cup. The goalkeeper is MANUEL BENTO (38 on June 25) with ZE BETO (26) as his deputy.

JOAO PINTO (24) has established himself well at right-back; in the
centre are the experienced LIMA PEREIRA (34), FREDERICO
(29), OLIVIERA (27), EURICO (30); while at left-back is INACIO
(31). There is a wealth of talent in midfield with JAIME PACHECO
(27) being a tireless worker, as is the star of the side CARLOS
MANUEL (27), ANTONIO SOUSA (28), the star of the future
FUTRE (20) and the gypsy-like bemuser CHALANA (27), who has
been playing in France during the last two seasons – injuries permit-
ting. In the attack are JORDAO (34 on August 9) who also has
suffered recently from injury, DIAMANTINO (26) who likes to rove
on the wings and FERNANDO GOMES (30) who has been very
difficult to prevent scoring goals. Indeed, he scored five of the 12
Portuguese goals, the next highest scorer being CARLOS MANUEL
with three.

England

*Football Association founded 1863. Joined FIFA 1905–20, 1924–28,
1946.*

Previous appearances: 1950, 1954 (Quarter-finalists), 1958, 1962
(Quarter-finalists), 1966 (Winners), 1970 (Quarter-finalists) and
1982.

Present tournament: Headed European Group 3 with 12 points from
8 games against NORTHERN IRELAND (1–0 away and 0–0
home), RUMANIA (0–0 away and 1–1 at home), FINLAND (5–0 at
home and 1–1 away) and TURKEY (8–0 away and 5–0 at home).
The only unbeaten side in Europe.

The manager and players: BOBBY ROBSON (52) who succeeded
RON GREENWOOD after the last World Cup, has been fortunate
enough to make use of several players who played in Spain. The
goalkeeper is still PETER SHILTON (36), GARY BAILEY (27) and
CHRIS WOODS (26) being his deputies, while KENNY SANSOM
(27) and TERRY BUTCHER (27) are still in the defence. Although
England let in fewer goals than any other European country (merely
2), the positions at the centre of the defence have still not been settled.
Those in contention are the tall and speedy MARK WRIGHT (22),
TERRY FENWICK (26) who has recently been scoring more than a
few goals, the resolute ALVIN MARTIN (27), DAVE WATSON (24),
and GARY STEVENS (23 on March 27 who has emerged recently

as a very promising right-back, with VIV ANDERSON (29) as his deputy. There is much talent in midfield with BRYAN ROBSON (29) and RAY WILKINS (29) both having played in the previous World Cup, the luxuriant skills of GLENN HODDLE (28) being allowed at last to impose themselves. The determined PETER REID (30 on June 20) and the gifted PAUL BRACEWELL (24 on July 19) have been selected recently, and others who might appear are RICKY HILL (27) and GORDON COWANS (27), who is having a grand season after his transfer a year ago from Aston Villa to Bari in Italy. The Everton pair of TREVOR STEVEN (22) and GARY LINEKER (25) have been in incisive form lately, the latter scoring goals by the handful, while the fearsome MARK HATELEY (24) and the speedy KERRY DIXON (24) are two impressive central strikers. CHRIS WADDLE (25) and JOHN BARNES (22) have shown themselves to be gifted lieutenants, the latter the scorer of a stupendous solo goal in the Maracana against Brazil on 10 June 1984. PAUL WALSH (23) has been in glorious form for Liverpool, PETER BEARDSLEY (25) has impressed when he has been selected and the experienced TONY WOODCOCK (30) has recently returned to form. Of the 21 goals ROBSON scored 5 and HATELEY 4.

The Federation (FIFA) has set May 23 as the final date for the nominations of players for the World Cup in Mexico. Unlike earlier World Cup matches, all twenty-two nominees may now occupy the areas next to the touch-line assigned to each side.

9 SOME OF THE BEST PLAYERS ON VIEW

Carlos AGUILERA (Uruguay). Born 21 September 1964, Aguilera is a fast and tricky forward who was first selected when he was 18.

Giancarlo ANTOGNONI (Italy). Born 1 April 1954, he was first selected in December 1974. A regular choice until seriously injured in November 1981, he made a spirited recovery and shone in the 1982 World Cup Finals. But 'Injury' must be his middle name since it was only in November 1985 that he played his first League game since breaking a leg in February 1984 and his admirers throughout the world sincerely hope that he will be chosen for the Italian squad on this occasion.

Salah ASSAD (Algeria). Born 30 August 1958, he played incisively in all three of Algeria's matches during the 1982 tournament and recently has been on very sharp form.

Joel BATS (France). Born 4 January 1957, Bats is a goalkeeper who gives great confidence to his defence – unlike several of his predecessors. Chosen regularly since September 1983, he went on to play in the European Nations Championship and should be the French goalkeeper for several years to come.

Lakhdar BELLOUMI (Algeria). Born 29 December 1958, Belloumi was voted African Footballer of 1981 and the 1982 World Cup Finals brought his attacking midfield skills to a much wider audience. Completely recovered from breaking his leg in March 1984 in a match against Libya in Tripoli.

Tadj BENSAOULA (Algeria). Born 1 December 1954, he is a vastly-experienced attacker who scores frequently.

Manuel BENTO (Portugal). Born 25 June 1948, Bento is a very flamboyant and experienced goalkeeper but one who can have 'off days'.

Oleg BLOKHIN (USSR). Born 5 November 1952, clever and experienced, he possesses a fearsome shot. Elected European Footballer of the Year for 1975, he is now used to playing rather deeper, where he is always busy setting up moves, and will seek to improve on his disappointing showing during the 1982 World Cup.

Zbigniew BONIEK (Poland). Born 3 March 1956, the 1978 World Cup brought Boniek to the front of the stage with all his skill. He is an indispensable member of the present-day Polish team and has great speed coupled with a talent for making very incisive passes. Signed by the Italian champions, Juventus, in April 1982 and now with Roma.

Claudio BORGHI (Argentina). Born 28 September 1964, Borghi is the latest in the line of young central strikers that have become available in the past few seasons, and possibly the most skilful. Ramon Diaz and Pedro Pasculli are trying their luck in the harsh world of Italian football.

Maxime BOSSIS (France). Born 26 June 1955, Bossis now plays as sweeper having formerly been a decisive left-back. A hard winner of the ball he is also skilful at helping to set up attacks.

Ian BRIDGE (Canada). Born 18 September 1959, a tall centre-back who has been improving with every season and recently spent some time playing with La Chaux de Fonds in Switzerland.

Jorge BURRUCHUGA (Argentina). Born 9 August 1962, Burruchuga is an attacking midfield player of great talent who moved to play in France during July 1985.

Terry BUTCHER (England). Born 28 December 1958 in Singapore, he played his first game as sweeper for England against Australia in May 1980, performed outstandingly during the last World Cup and has since become an automatic choice for his country.

Emilio BUTRAGENO (Spain). Born 22 July 1963 and nicknamed 'El Buitre' (The Vulture), Butrageno has been one of the sensations of Spanish football during the last two seasons. He possesses the most astonishing skills and has an excellent football brain. He plays his club football for Real Madrid between Hugo Sanchez of Mexico and Jorge Valdano of Argentina, and well enough to displace Carlos Santillana.

Wilmar CABRERA (Uruguay). Born 31 July 1959, Cabrera is a noted header of the ball who moved from Millionaros of Bogota to Spain in 1984.

Antonio CABRINI (Italy). Born 8 October 1957, Cabrini won his place in the Italian side for the first game of the 1978 World Cup and has played ever since. A tight marker, he loves making runs into the attack.

Santos CARLOS MANUEL (Portugal). Born 15 January 1958, he must be one of the most effective midfield players in Europe and although his role is mainly defensive, he can make the occasional piercing move into the attack (for example, his goal against West Germany in Stuttgart).

Antonio Carlos CEREZO (Brazil). Born 21 April 1955, he now plays in Italy, has been not unfavourably compared to previous stars such as Didì and Gerson, but has recently been under the knife of the surgeon.

Jan CEULEMANS (Belgium). Born 28 February 1957, he is a tall and strong-running forward who makes penetrating runs into the attack.

CHA Bum-Kun (South Korea). Born 25 May 1953, he moved in 1978 to play for Eintracht Frankfurt in West Germany and is still there, playing for Beyer Leverkausen.

Fernando Albino CHALANA (Portugal). Born 10 February 1959, he was first selected as a substitute when he was 17 but since then has won a regular place as a deep-lying central prompter for the attacks of the side. He has been playing in France for the last two seasons but has also experienced many injury problems.

Alexandr CHIVADZE (USSR). Born 8 April 1955, Chivadze is a cultured sweeper of the side who is skilful in making attacking runs into the midfield. He was first selected in April 1980, since when he has become an indispensable figure in the defence.

CHOI Soon-Ho (South Korea). Born 10 January 1962, Choi is a svelte and rapid striker whose skills have interested many European teams.

Bruno CONTI (Italy). Born 13 March 1955, Conti made his first appearance as a substitute in October 1980, was undoubtedly one of the stars of the 1982 Italian triumph in the World Cup finals with his intelligent and incisive play on the wings, but is now vying with Pietro Fanna for a place in the team.

Jorge DA SILVA (Uruguay). Born 11 December 1961, Da Silva is a goal-making forward who moved to play in Spain during the 1984/5 season.

Kenny DALGLISH (Scotland). Born 4 March 1951, and the only Scottish player to have been capped over 100 times, he came to join Liverpool from Celtic in the summer of 1977 soon after Keegan had left for Hamburg. He fitted into that side marvellously, and thrills the Kop at each game. A very skilful striker of the ball, Dalglish possesses that rare gift of being able to turn through 180 degrees whenever he's standing with his back to goal, and always proves a very difficult player to mark.

Renat DASSAEV (USSR). Dassaev, who was born 12 April 1957, first played in September 1979 and has made the goalkeeping position his own. Brave and agile, he has quick reflexes and is in the line of great Russian keepers such as Lev Yashin, which means that he is among the best in the world.

Hugo DE LEON (Uruguay). Born 27 February 1958, De Leon is a tall and straight-backed stopper who defends extremely rigorously and although he did not participate in any games in the qualifying round, has a wealth of experience and could well be used in Mexico.

Lajos DETARI (Hungary). Born 24 April 1963, Detari is a phenomenon, the nub of the side, in addition to being a goal-scorer, and invites comparisons with Jozef Bozsik, captain of the celebrated side of the Fifties.

Dariusz DZIEKANOWSKI (Poland). Born 30 September 1962, he is undoubtedly one of the new stars of Polish football, being quick-silver fast and also powerful in the air.

Preben ELKJAER-LARSEN (Denmark). Born 11 September 1957, he took his talents as a goal-scorer to Italy after the 1984 European Championships.

Paulo Roberto FALCAO (Brazil). Born 16 October 1953, he joined Roma in the middle of 1980. His class told at once and he was called back by Tele Santana to help the cause of his country in the 1982 World Cup. Injury struck during the 1984–5 season, at the end of which he was transferred back to Brazil and Sao Paulo but he finished the season in great style overseeing the development of younger players such as the 22-year-old Muller the 20-year-old Silas and the 22-year-old left-winger Sidnei.

Ubaldo FILLOL (Argentina). Born 21 July 1950, he was goalkeeper to the victorious Argentinian side in the 1978 World Cup. Indeed, he was selected in the previous tournament and throughout the 1982 competition proved to be absolutely first class. Moved in July 1985 to play in Spain for Atletico Madrid.

Karl-Heinz FÖRSTER (West Germany). Born 25 July 1958, he won his first selection in October 1978 and has been a firm choice as stopper ever since.

Enzo FRANCESCOLI (Uruguay). Born 12 November 1961, Francescoli could be one of the stars of the tournament. He has been sought by many clubs in Italy and Spain and is an attacking midfield-player whom even Juan Schiaffino estimates as being among the best Uruguayan players he has seen in the last twenty years. A prolific goal-scorer Francescoli plays for River Plate in Buenos Aires and was South American Player of the Year for 1984.

Paulo Jorge dos Santos FUTRE (Portugal). Born 1 March 1965, Futre is unquestionably the most promising Portuguese player since the time of the triumph in the 1966 World Cup. He was first for the national side when he was just over seventeen and a half – taking the honour of being the youngest-ever to gain that particular distinction from his midfield companion, Chalana.

Imre GARABA (Hungary). Born 29 July 1958 Garaba is a formidably resolute central defender who was first capped in 1980 and has played regularly ever since.

GEOVANI Silva (Brazil). Born 6 April 1964, he is a forward of tremendous gifts, was instrumental in Brazil's victory in the 1983 World Youth Cup and could be a sensation in Mexico.

Eric GERETS (Belgium). Born 18 May 1954, Gerets began his playing career as a centre-forward, but switched in 1973 to playing in the defence and is now a most effective right-back. He has experienced several unfortunate twists of fate in the last year or two, but is now playing as well as ever.

Alain GIRESSE (France). Born 2 August 1952, Giresse is a small, busy midfield player who really came into prominence just prior to the 1982 World Cup, in which he performed outstandingly.

Fernando GOMES (Portugal). Born 29 September 1956, Gomes is the man who has the happy instinct of the born goal-scorer, and has been scoring regularly since he first began playing senior football when he was 18.

Mark HATELEY (England). Born 7 November 1961, Hateley was transferred by Portsmouth to A. C. Milan in July 1984, just after he had been first selected by England. Powerful in the air, Mexico could bring the best out of him.

Pat JENNINGS (Northern Ireland). Born June 12 1945, Jennings is the most capped player in the world (or soon will be!) and for the past decade has played with a high sense of his craft, at times making saves which are truly breathtaking. He played an outstanding game against Spain in 1982 and relishes the opportunity of being faced by the Brazilians for the first time on his 41st birthday.

Rui Manuel JORDAO (Portugal). Born 9 August 1952, Jordao has been unfortunate with injuries lately but when fully fit teams up excellently alongside Fernando Gomez.

Gama JUNIOR Leovegildo Lins (Brazil). Born 29 June 1954, Junior moved from Flamengo to the Italian side of Torino in June 1984, and switched from being an attacking left-back into a powerful player in midfield.

KIM Jong-Boo (South Korea). Born 3 January 1965, Kim is a quick and shrewd forward who was a member of the South Korean team which came fourth in the World Youth Cup three years ago and has all the talent to cause many problems in Mexico.

KRIMAU Merry (Morocco). Born 13 January 1955, Krimau has been playing in France for the past 11 years, is notably good when the ball is in the air and has been very much on form during the past few months.

Michel LAUDRUP (Denmark). Born 15 June 1964, he is one of three Danish internationals currently playing in Italy (the others being Klaus Berggreen and Preben Elkjaer-Larsen) and will undoubtedly be a great threat to the defences of West Germany, Uruguay and Scotland. Among others?

Soren LERBY (Denmark). Born 1 February 1958, he is a gloriously gifted midfield player who possesses acute vision to go with his left-foot shooting.

Tino LETTIERI (Canada). Born 27 September 1957 in Bari, Italy, Lettieri has been the first-choice goalkeeper in Canada since 1980, making up with his agility for his lack of height.

Pierre LITTBARSKI (West Germany). Born 16 April 1960, Littbarski made his debut in the national side on 14 October 1981 and scored two of the goals in the 3–1 victory over Austria in Vienna. A wispish player down both flanks he also cunningly times his attacks in front of goal.

Antonio MACEDA (Spain). Born 26 May 1957, Maceda is a dominant *libero* who played outstandingly in the 1984 European Championships and forms a very powerful central defence along with the rugged Goiecochea.

Rabah MADJER (Algeria). Born 15 December 1958, Madjer is the man who scored the first of Algeria's goals against West Germany in the 2–0 victory during the last World Cup, and has taken his talents this year to play in Portugal.

Diego MARADONA (Argentina). Born 31 October 1960, he won his first cap on 29 February 1977 – 18 months before the World Cup, for which he was not chosen. It was a good thing for Menotti that he won the Cup without the infant prodigy but the Argentinian manager didn't want to upset his settled side by taking in a player of such varied talents. When Maradona has the ball he seems to be a god: a god capable of breath-taking dribbling, lethal shooting or a telling pass; a genius that can often transfix opposing players. Although voted South American Footballer of the Year for 1979 and 1980 he was disappointing in the 1982 World Cup and will be looking to perform much better in Mexico. Knees willing.

Alan McDONALD (Northern Ireland). Born 12 October 1963, McDonald couldn't have asked for a harsher christening – away to Rumania in a match that his team simply had to win to remain in the competition. Not a bit daunted by the prospect, he gave a performance of total assurance in the middle of the defence and surely will be a member of the Northern Ireland team for years to come.

Sammy McILROY (Northern Ireland). Born 2 August 1954, McIlroy has become one of the best attacking midfield players in Britain, making pin-point passes that can split the opposition, as well as some telling runs. He won his first cap in 1972.

Willie MILLER (Scotland). Born 2 May 1955, and a one-club man (Aberdeen), Willie Miller was first selected as long ago as June 1975, but over the last six years has become a regular choice in the middle of the defence alongside his club-mate Ally McLeish.

Stojco MLADENOV (Bulgaria). Born 24 April 1957, Mladenov is a sharp and speedy attacker who has been selected on more than 65 occasions.

Josef MLYNARCZYK (Poland). Born 20 September 1953, he is a thoroughly competent goalkeeper who joined the Portuguese champions, Porto, since his former club of Bastia in France could not pay the players' wages.

Jan MOLBY (Denmark). Born 4 July 1963, Molby brought his talents to Liverpool and after a season becoming used to the pace of the English game struck really handsome form during the 1985/6 season and could become one of the personalities of the 1986 World Cup.

Charlie NICHOLAS (Scotland). Born in Glasgow 30 December 1960, he won his first cap in March 1983, moved South from Celtic to join Arsenal during the summer of 1983 and, after a very long period adjusting to the different tempo of the game in England, is at last starting to recapture that brilliant form of his early years.

Jesper OLSEN (Denmark). Born 20 March 1961, Olsen brought his talents to Manchester United before the 1984/5 season and has been thrilling many people with his tigerish running down both wings.

Tibor NYILASI (Hungary). Born 18 January 1955, he was formerly the real play-maker of the Hungarian team. Perceptive vision, excellent control and the ability to make surging runs into the attack have helped to make this tall and large-boned player one of the most courted in Europe.

Martin O'NEILL (Northern Ireland). Born 1 March 1952, he was first selected for a full international in March 1973 since when he has been a regular choice in midfield. Billy Bingham is not alone in hoping that he has fully recovered from an injury which kept him out for much of the 1985/86 season.

José OSCAR Bernardi (Brazil). Born 20 June 1954. Oscar played as a central defender in all of Brazil's games during the 1978 and 1982 finals. A well-built stopper, he is still mobile enough to make good use of the ball after it has been won.

Daniel PASSARELLA (Argentina). Born 25 May 1953, he was captain and sweeper of the team that won the 1978 World Cup. A good man not to meet when alone on an attack, he signed for the

Italian club of Fiorentina after the last World Cup where he has
settled down imposingly after a nervous start.

Michel PLATINI (France). Born 21 June 1955 and one of the most
gifted players in the world, Platini was first selected in March 1976
since when he has been a regular member of the side. A real specialist
with free kicks, he loves to make telling runs from midfield into the
attack. After the 1982 World Cup he was transferred from St Etienne
to the Italian champions, Juventus, for whom he scores regularly. He
was voted European Footballer of the Year for 1983, 1984 and 1985.

Oleg PROTASOV (USSR). Born 14 February 1960, Protasov is an
athletic striker who has recently come into the Russian side to play
alongside the legendary Oleg Blokhin, and has scored approximately a
goal in every other game.

Venancio RAMOS (Uruguay). Born 20 June 1959, he was selected
when he was only 20 for his country for whom he provides width on
the wings, and moved from Penarol to the French club of Lens.
Scored the crucial penalty that gave Uruguay a 2–1 victory in the final
game of their qualifying Group against close-rivals, Chile.

Bryan ROBSON (England). Born 11 January 1957, he won his first
cap in February 1980 and was the only man to play in all of England's
eight games in the qualifying tournament for the 1982 World Cup, in
the finals of which he performed outstandingly. One who anticipates
cleverly and uses the ball intelligently, he can look forward to another
World Cup with the knowledge that he is one of the foremost midfield
players in Europe.

Dominique ROCHETEAU (France). Born 14 January 1955, he was
first selected on 3 September 1975 as a right wing but now tends to be
more of a central attacker.

Rodolfo Sergio RODRIGUEZ (Uruguay). Born 20 January 1956, he
has been a regular choice for the last five years and in the Copa De Ora
competition (held in Montevideo between all the previous winners of
the World Cup) conceded only one goal in three games and that from
a dubious penalty.

Julio Cesar ROMERO (Paraguay). Born 28 August 1960, Romero is
a midfield player who plays his club football for Fluminese in Brazil
and is undoubtedly the springboard of his side's attacks. He was voted
South American Footballer of the Year for 1985.

Paolo ROSSI (Italy). Born 23 September 1956, Rossi is a central striker of acute sharpness in the penalty box, one who can score from the most narrow of angles. First selected in December 1977, he was a star of the World Cup Finals of the year afterwards. He totally recovered from having been absented from football for two years, as of April 1980, for having been implicated in a match-fixing scandal and was highest scorer in the 1982 World Cup. It would surprise no-one if his third appearance in a World Cup Finals was also a triumph. He was voted European Footballer of the Year for 1982.

Karl-Heinz RUMMENIGGE (West Germany). Born 25 September 1955, he is a blond-haired winger who likes to surge in on goal and score himself. He began to play for Bayern Munich in 1974 and was first capped by his country on 6 October 1976. He took part in the 1978 and 1982 World Cups and is now playing most effectively for both club and country. He was voted European Footballer of the Year for 1980 and 1981 and joined Internazionale of Milan before the 1984/5 season, playing alongside Sandro Altobelli.

Kenny SANSOM (England). Born 26 September 1958, Sansom is a left-back of high potential. Stocky in build he made his debut for England in the o–o draw against Wales in May 1979 and has made the position his own.

Harold SCHUMACHER (West Germany). Born 6 March 1954, he came into the side for the 1980 European Championships and has made the goalkeeping position his own with his sure handling, complete confidence when coming out to deal with crosses, and his intelligent distribution.

Bernd SCHUSTER (West Germany). Born 22 December 1959, he was another influential figure in that West Germany victory with his fearless and skilful running in midfield. Soon after, he was transferred to Barcelona and although injured just before the last World Cup, in which his talents could have been crucial, everyone who wishes to see West Germany perform well in Mexico must be praying that he takes part.

Vicenzo SCIFO (Belgium). Born 19 February 1966 to Sicilian parents, Scifo was first selected to play for Belgium on June 6 1984 and has since very much become the guiding-light of their midfield.

Gaetano SCIREA (Italy). Born 25 May 1953, he was first selected as *libero* on 30 December 1977, played outstandingly during the 1978 and 1982 World Cups, and has proved to be a worthy successor to Giacinto Facchetti.

Peter SHILTON (England). Born 18 September 1949, he won his first cap in November 1970, succeeded Gordon Banks as the England goalkeeper after the latter was injured in a road accident in 1972, played regularly until July 1974 and since then has shared the role with Ray Clemence. He played outstandingly well in the 1982 World Cup and has made the goalkeeping position very much his own under Bobby Robson's management.

Allan SIMONSEN (Denmark). Born 15 December 1952, he was elected in front of Kevin Keegan as European Footballer of the Year for 1977. He was transferred to Spanish football in the middle of 1979 and has brought his sharp finishing, his talent for playing off quick one-twos and his all-round feeling for the game to increase the enjoyment of Spanish fans.

Wlodzimierz SMOLAREK (Poland). Born 16 July 1957, he was most effective in the 1982 World Cup, but since then has suffered numerous injuries in addition to loss of form, and the Polish manager, Antoni Piechnizek, will be hoping that he has totally recovered by the spring.

Graeme SOUNESS (Scotland). Born 6 May 1953, he came south to join Tottenham Hotspur when he was 16, was transferred to Middlesbrough and then Liverpool. He played in only Scotland's final game in the 1978 World Cup but is now a regular member of their midfield.

Gordon STRACHAN (Scotland). Born 9 February 1957, he was first selected in 1980 and has always played with vision and bite, setting up attacks.

Marco TARDELLI (Italy). Born 24 September 1954, he was first selected as right-back in April 1976, moved forward to play in midfield just before the 1978 World Cup, and is a permanent member of the Italian team.

Mohamed TIMOUMI (Morocco). Born 15 January 1960, Timoumi is a most elegant midfield player, precise in his passing and eager to score goals. Was elected African 'Footballer of the Year' for 1985.

Carl VALENTINE (Canada). Born 4 July 1958, he is a forward who has experienced valuable service in the English First Division.

Rudi VOLLER (West Germany). Born 13 April 1960, Voller has experienced a meteoric rise since joining Werder Bremen in 1982, becoming the top scorer of the season. Injury has cramped him of late, however, but when fit he makes an ideal partner for the more-experienced Rummenigge.

Norman WHITESIDE (Northern Ireland). Born 7 May 1965 and in the record books as the youngest player to take part in the Finals of a World Cup, he now plays an attacking role in midfield and scores frequently with fierce left-foot shots.

Ray WILKINS (England). Born 14 September 1956. Wilkins won his first cap in May 1976 when England beat Italy 3–2 in New York. He is a player of the highest talent, combines with Robson and Hoddle to make a feature of the right side of England's midfield, and can shoot strongly with either foot.

ZAKI (Morocco). Born as Ezaki Badou 2 April 1959, Zaki is among the stars of the team and only let through one goal in the eight qualifying matches played by Morocco.

ZICO (Brazil). Born as Arthur Artunes Coimbra on 3 March 1953, Zico was first capped in 1975. He experienced a most unhappy time in the 1978 World Cup and although the 1982 tournament brought the best out of him, a transfer to Italy proved to be complicated. He can, however, be a most thrilling player and will hope to perform well in Mexico, not least with his devastating free kicks. He was voted South American Player of the Year for 1977, 1981 and 1982.

Radoslav ZDRAVKOV (Bulgaria). Born 30 March 1956, he is a very experienced player who operates on the right side of midfield.

Wladyslaw ZMUDA (Poland). Born 6 June 1954, he has played in the centre of the defence ever since first being selected in October 1973. Calm and thoughtful he appears to be able to play the game at his own pace – a rare gift. Joined Verona in 1982 and has spent the last four years playing in Italian football.

10 MEXICO – THE RECORD, THE MANAGER, THE PLAYERS AND THE GROUNDS

Mexico's record in the World Cup is undistinguished. The country has qualified in 1930, 1950, 1954, 1958, 1962, 1966 and 1978 and acted as hosts for the tournament in 1970 (when it reached the Quarter-final stage). Those eight appearances have produced the following result:

P	W	D	L	F	A
24	3	4	17	21	62

Two of those three victories were gained in 1970, over El Salvador (4–0) and Belgium (1–0). In the 1978 tournament the record was disastrous since Mexico lost all three of its games – 1–3 to Tunisia, 0–6 to West Germany and 1–3 to Poland.

Home advantage should be a considerable help (particularly in a country that knows freakish conditions of heat as well as of altitude) but the pressures on the manager of a team playing at home in the World Cup are intense, as witnessed by the manager of Spain during the last tournament who, after Spain's pitiful showing in their five games, has been unable to return to management inside the game.

Since his appointment as manager to the national team at the end of 1982, the Yugoslav VELIBOR (BORA) MILUTINOVIC, has done everything possible to weld together the 20-odd players he has 'taken out' of Mexican club football. Born 7 September 1944, he played for the nearby team of Partizan Belgrade, winning a League Championship medal in 1965, before moving on to play in France with Nice and Monaco. He later moved to the Mexican club Universidad Nacional before retiring from playing in 1975. After experiencing success in coaching his club side, Milutinovic was appointed coach to the national side and has done much to alter the style of coaching, transforming it from the lazy, over-individualistic approach to one in which genuine team-work helps compensate for deficiencies in individual skill. He has arranged tours of Europe and South America in attempts to provide his players with wide experience, and below is a roster of those who will be expected to help make Mexico the third host country in four tournaments to experience success.

Javier AGUIRRE. Born 1 December 1958, he is a very skilful attacking midfield player who was called into the national set-up by Bora Milutinovic at the beginning of 1983.

Rafael AMADOR. Born 15 February 1959, he is a tall and more experienced left-back whose skills have long been recognised by Bora Milutinovic.

Tomas BOY. Born 28 June 1952, Boy is a very skilful midfield player who, whenever possible, likes to make darting runs into the attack.

Carlos de los COBOS. Born 6 December 1958, he is a skilful midfield player who is a regular member of the national party.

Francisco CHAVEZ. Born 6 July 1959, he is a defender who loves to make cunning breaks into the midfield.

Alejandro DOMINGUEZ. Born 9 November 1961, he is an attacking midfield player of great flair.

Miguel ESPANA. Born 31 January 1964, he is a midfield player who was called in from the club which Bora Milutinovic used to coach, UNAM.

Luis FLORES. Born 18 July 1961, a central striker in the team who has done his best to compensate for the absence of Hugo Sanchez and is highly regarded by his manager for his positional play and his opportunism.

Fernando Quirarte GUTTIEREZ. Born 17 May 1956, he is a tall and skilful central defender.

Carlos Olaf HEREDIA. Born 19 October 1957, Heredia makes up in his agility for what he lacks in acumen and his nervousness in coming out of the goalmouth.

Carlos HERMOSILLO. Born 24 August 1960, he is a new discovery who has come on markedly in confidence during the past two years.

Pablo LARIOS. Born 31 July 1960, Larios is a brave goalkeeper whom Milutinovic brought into the side when he became team manager.

Armando MANZO. Born 16 October 1958, he is the present stopper of the team and has been a member of the national squad since 1980.

Carlos MUNOZ. Born 8 September 1960, he is a defensive midfield player of great drive who has been brought into the team by Bora Milutinovic.

Manuel NEGRETE. Born 11 March 1960, he is a lightly-built but gutsy midfield player who likes to make incursions to the attack.

Hugo SANCHEZ. Born in Mexico City 11 July 1958, Hugo Sanchez is undoubtedly the most gifted Mexican footballer of his generation and must be at the top of his form as a striker if the host country is going to achieve notable results in the competition. First selected for the amateur side when he was only 16, he went on to play in the Montreal Olympics and two years later played in all three of Mexico's games during the 1978 World Cup. In 1981 he was transferred to Atletico Madrid in Spain, with whom he remained until July 1985 when he moved across to the more prestigious Real Madrid. At the finish of the 1984-85 season he was the leading goal-scorer in Spain, ahead of Jorge Valdano (17) and Steve Archibald (15) and Mexico will certainly look to him to use all the expertise he has acquired out-thinking tight defences in Europe during the last five years.

Raul SERVIN. Born 29 April 1963, he is a young, promising left-back.

Alfredo TENA. Born 21 November 1956, he is a very experienced sweeper who has a strong tackle and is good in the air. Played as stopper during the 1978 tournament.

Marco Alberto TREJO. Born 11 February 1956, Trejo is a right-back of great authority who was a member of the national squad as long ago as 1980.

The Grounds for the 86 World Cup

GROUP A:	MEXICO CITY (AZTEC) – 110,000
	MEXICO CITY (OLYMPIC) – 72,000
	PUEBLA – 46,416
GROUP B:	MEXICO CITY (AZTEC) – 110,000
	TOLUCA – 36,612
GROUP C:	LEON – 30,531
	IRAPUATO – 31,336
GROUP D:	GUADALAJARA (JALISCO) – 66,193
	GUADALAJARA (MARCH THE THIRD) – 30,015
GROUP E:	NEZAHUALCOYOTL – 34,536
	QUERÉTARO (new) – 38,576
GROUP F:	MONTERREY (UNIVERSITA) – 43,780
	MONTERREY (TECHNOLOGICO) – 33,805

11 COMPLETE FIRST ROUND DRAW

The First Round Draw was made on 15 December by five-year-old LUIS JAVIER BARROSO CANEDO whose mother MONICA MARIA was 12 when she made the draw for the 1970 World Cup. His grandfather is GUILLERMO CANEDO, president of the organising committee and vice-president of FIFA.

G.M.T. 7 HOURS LATER

GROUP A
Mexico City Aztec Stadium
Olympic Stadium
Puebla

MAY 31	(A)	Italy	Bulgaria	*(Mexico City 12.00 noon)*
JUNE 2	(O)	Argentina	South Korea	*(Mexico City 12.00 noon)*
JUNE 5		Italy	Argentina	*(Puebla 12.00 noon)*
JUNE 5	(O)	Bulgaria	South Korea	*(Mexico City 4.00 p.m.)*
JUNE 10		Italy	South Korea	*(Puebla 12.00 noon)*
JUNE 10	(O)	Bulgaria	Argentina	*(Mexico City 12.00 noon)*

GROUP B
Mexico City Aztec Stadium
Toluca

JUNE 3	(A)	Mexico	Belgium	*(Mexico City 12.00 noon)*
JUNE 4		Paraguay	Iraq	*(Toluca 12.00 noon)*
JUNE 7	(A)	Mexico	Paraguay	*(Mexico City 12.00 noon)*
JUNE 8		Belgium	Iraq	*(Toluca 12.00 noon)*
JUNE 11	(A)	Mexico	Iraq	*(Mexico City 12.00 noon)*
JUNE 11		Belgium	Paraguay	*(Toluca 12.00 noon)*

GROUP C
Leon
Irapuato

JUNE 1	France	Canada	*(Leon 4.00 p.m.)*
JUNE 2	Soviet Union	Hungary	*(Irapuato 12.00 noon)*
JUNE 5	France	Soviet Union	*(Leon 12.00 noon)*
JUNE 6	Canada	Hungary	*(Irapuato 12.00 noon)*
JUNE 9	France	Hungary	*(Leon 12.00 noon)*
JUNE 9	Canada	Soviet Union	*(Irapuato 12.00 noon)*

GROUP D
Guadalajara Jalisco Stadium
March 3 Stadium

JUNE 1	(J)	Brazil	Spain	*(Guadalajara 12.00 noon)*
JUNE 3	(M)	Algeria	Northern Ireland	*(Guadalajara 12.00 noon)*
JUNE 6	(J)	Brazil	Algeria	*(Guadalajara 12.00 noon)*
JUNE 7	(M)	Spain	Northern Ireland	*(Guadalajara 12.00 noon)*
JUNE 12	(J)	Brazil	Northern Ireland	*(Guadalajara 12.00 noon)*
JUNE 12	(M)	Spain	Algeria	*(Guadalajara 12.00 noon)*

GROUP E
Mexico City Neza Stadium
Querétaro

JUNE 4		West Germany	Uruguay	*(Querétaro 12.00 noon)*
JUNE 4	(N)	Scotland	Denmark	*(Mexico City 4.00 p.m.)*
JUNE 8		Scotland	West Germany	*(Querétaro 12.00 noon)*
JUNE 8	(N)	Uruguay	Denmark	*(Mexico City 4.00 p.m.)*
JUNE 13		West Germany	Denmark	*(Querétaro 12.00 noon)*
JUNE 13	(N)	Uruguay	Scotland	*(Mexico City 12.00 noon)*

GROUP F
Monterrey University Stadium
Technological Stadium

JUNE 2	(U)	Poland	Morocco	*(Monterrey 4.00 p.m.)*
JUNE 3	(T)	England	Portugal	*(Monterrey 4.00 p.m.)*
JUNE 6	(T)	England	Morocco	*(Monterrey 4.00 p.m.)*
JUNE 7	(U)	Poland	Portugal	*(Monterrey 4.00 p.m.)*
JUNE 11	(U)	England	Poland	*(Monterrey 4.00 p.m.)*
JUNE 11	(T)	Morocco	Portugal	*(Monterrey 4.00 p.m.)*

Second Round

JUNE 15: Winners of Group B (.............) v third-placed in Group A, C or D (...............) at Aztec Stadium, Mexico City, 12.00 noon. Winner (...............) will be number 8 for Quarter-final schedule. Winners of Group C (...............) v third-placed in Group A, B or F (...............) at Leon, 4.00 p.m. Winner (...............): 4.

JUNE 16: Winners of Group A (.............) v third-placed in Group C, D or E (...............) at Puebla, 4.00 p.m. Winner (...............): 1. Winners of Group D (...............) v third-placed in Group B, E or F (..............) at Jalisco Stadium, Guadalajara, 12.00 noon. Winner (...............): 5.

JUNE 17: Runners-up in Group A (.............) v runners-up in Group C (...............) at Olympic Stadium, Mexico City, 12.00 noon. Winner (...............): 6. Winners of Group F (..............) v runners-up in Group E (...............) at University Stadium, Monterrey, 4.00 p.m. Winner (...............): 7.

JUNE 18: Runners-up in Group F (.............) v runners-up in Group B (...............) at Aztec Stadium, Mexico City, 12.00 noon. Winner (...............): 2. Winners of Group E (...............) v runners-up in Group D (..............) at Querétaro, 4.00 p.m. Winner (...............): 3.

Quarter-Finals

June 21: 5 (...............) v 6 (...............) at Jalisco Stadium, Guadalajara, 12.00 noon. Winner (...............): C for Semi-finals. 7 (...............) v 8 (...............) at University Stadium, Monterrey, 4.00 p.m. Winner (...............): D.

June 22: 3 (...............) v 4 (...............) at Puebla, 4.00 p.m. Winner (...............): B 1 (...............) v 2 (...............) at Aztec Stadium, Mexico City, 12.00 noon. Winner (...............): A.

Semi-Finals

JUNE 25: A (...............) v B (...............) at Aztec Stadium, Mexico City 4.00 p.m. Winner: .... C (...............) v D (...............) at Jalisco Stadium, Guadalajara, 12.00 noon. Winner: ....

Third Place Match
June 28: 12.00 noon at Puebla.

FINAL

June 29: at Aztec Stadium, Mexico City, 12.00 noon. The competing countries are:

.... versus ....

The players are:

....
....
....
....
....
....
....
....
....
....
....

The men who will officiate are:

Europe: H. Brummeier (Austria), A. Ponnet (Belgium), B. Dotsche (Bulgaria), V. Christov (Czechoslovakia), G. Courtney (England), J. Quiniou (France), S. Kirschen (E. Germany), V. Roth (West Germany), L. Nemeth (Hungary), A. Snoddy (N. Ireland), L. Agnolin (Italy), J. Keizer (Netherlands), I. Igna (Romania), B. McGinlay (Scotland), V. S. Arminio (Spain), E. Fredriksson (Sweden), A. Daina (Switzerland), V. Butenko (USSR), Z. Petrovic (Yugoslavia).

South America: C. A. Esposito (Argentina), R. A. Filho (Brazil), H. Silva (Chile), J. D. Palacio (Colombia), G. E. Roa (Paraguay), J. L. M. Bazan (Uruguay).

CONCACAF: B. U. Morera (C. Rica), R. Mendez Molina (Guatemala), A. M. Ramirez (Mexico), D. S. Socha (US).

Asia: S. Takada (Japan), F. K. Al-Shanar (Saudi Arabia), J. Al-Sharif (Syria).

Africa: I. Traore (Mali), E. Piconackong (Mauritius), A. Ben Naceur (Tunisia).

Oceania: C. Bambridge (Australia).

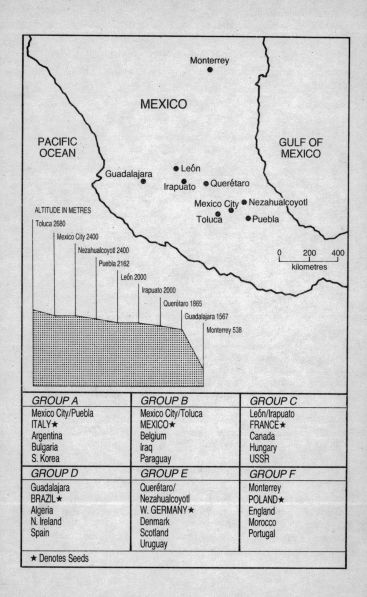